High Shelf

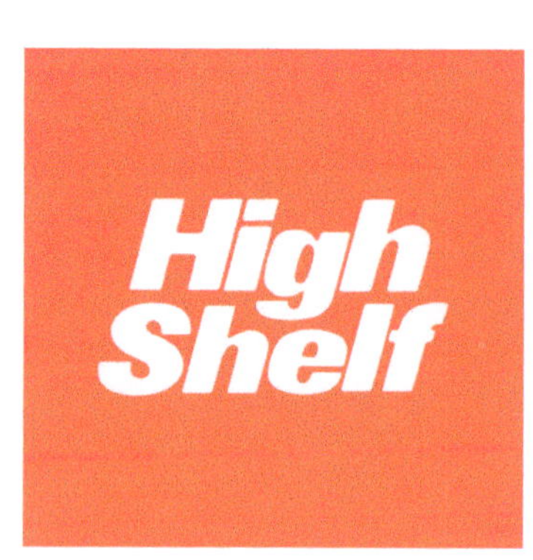

High Shelf XLI April 2022
Portland, Oregon.
Copyright 2022, High Shelf Press

ISBN: 978-1-952869-60-0

Cover Image by Justin Snyder

High Shelf XLI

April 2022

"... Even birds know

Who is prey

Who is predator... "

Nancy Klepsch

“…He knocked at 3 a.m with no promises, we had a drink,
he took my dress, the wall he pinned me up against was cloud…”
Emily Rosie

Table Of Contents

No Nature Allowed

Margie B. Klein

Humans in the suburbs. They said no more nature. They wanted the neighborhood to be clean, uniform, and perfect. They didn't like all those 'wild' things. Too messy, too tangled, too many problems. And animals? Fear and disgust dictated that they could do without them. The homeowner association said that residents could have lawns of rock, accented by artificial statuary and trees. Ground must be covered by black plastic before putting rock down. Water outside the home was taboo and could not be seen. They may, however, construct a mirage of blue-green glass pieces. No animals outside the home, either. Pets must be kept indoors at all times and organic waste cleanly contained and unseen when disposed of. Live plants are allowed inside the home, not outside, even under patios. Weeds must be removed immediately. Walkways and driveways will be kept clear of any debris or blockage. Approved landscape materials to include concrete, stone, rock, gravel and other hardscape materials. Pests in the category of insects and animals must be repelled, killed or otherwise isolated from the landscape. Animal deterrents to include wire stakes, metal screening, and chemical formulations, but no facsimiles of animals. Solar panels, either on the roof or ground, will not be allowed in any circumstance. All roofs to be tiled according to regulation. There will neither be any depictions of wild nature in the yard, on the brick walls, or on the house.

And Nature laughed. Good luck finding me when you need me again, she thought.

From the Ground Up

Adrienne Wenne

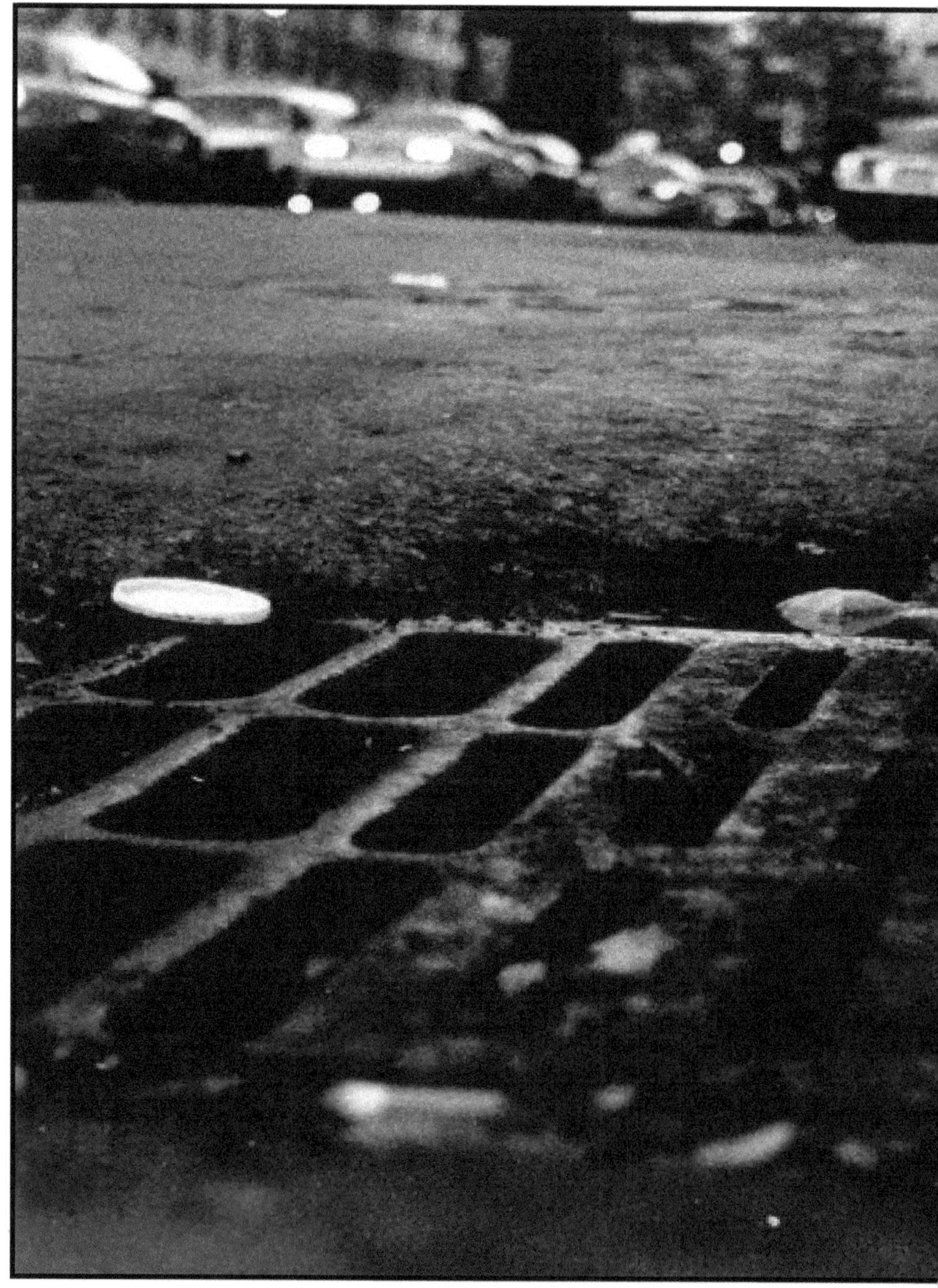

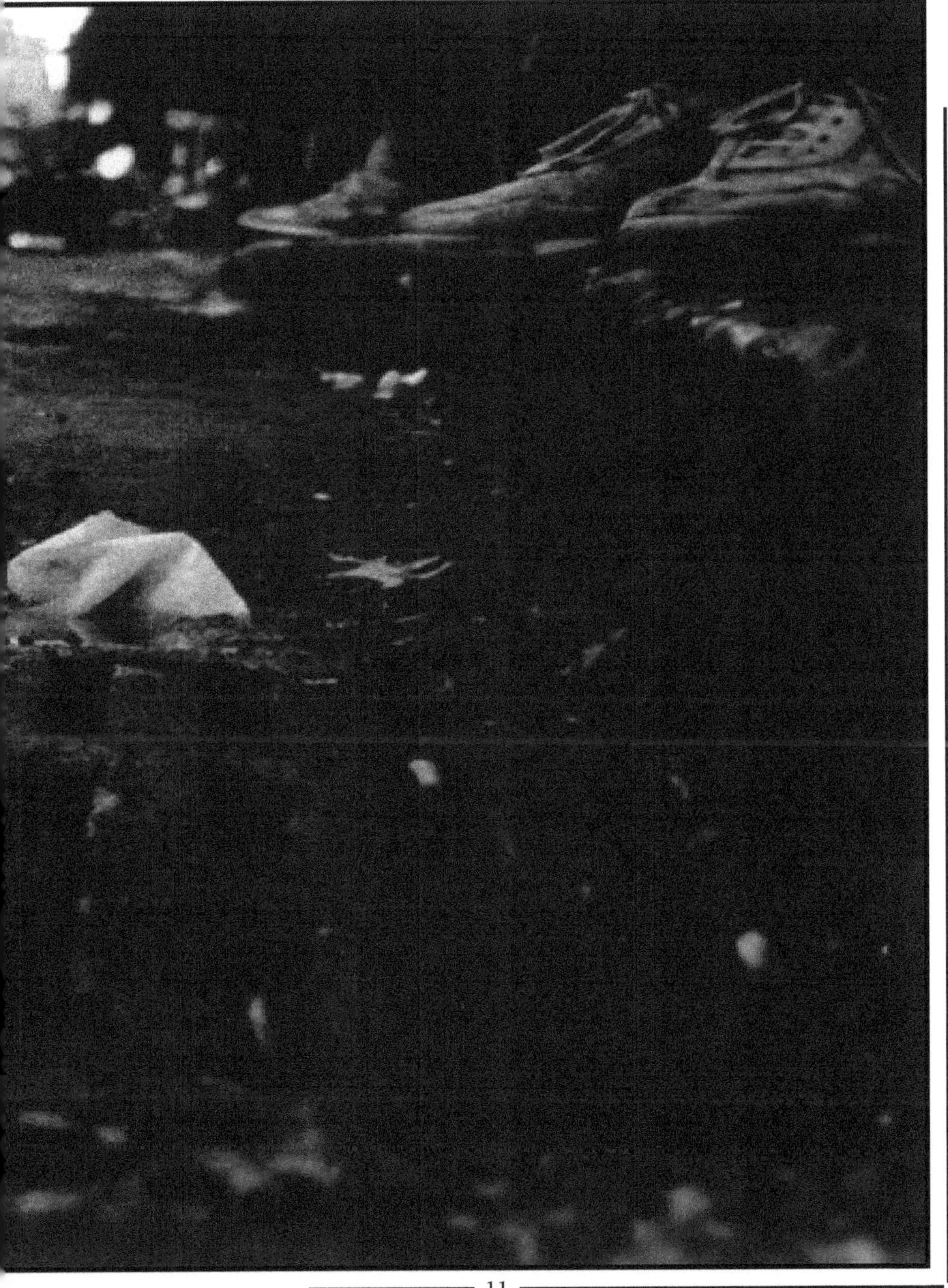

Medusa

Emily Griffin

You're frozen for me now, my gem.
No more rushing fists. No more screaming.
I've turned you to stone.

Now I love you perfectly, forever.

You could never hurt me, my gem.
No more shields or flags flying from masts;
you're a stone of the earth, no nation to speak of.

No one to cry out to in a cave with someone like me.

Shine for me so still, little gem.
I stare at you so close and learn your life.
This was meant as a curse but I love it.

I remember them singing as they beat me, little gem.

Beautiful statues never hurt anyone.
Besides, warriors who run off seeking Medusa
are all asking for it anyway.

The Sidewalk is Parallel to the Sky

Josh Feit

because when you're living in a city

— parallel is what?

Sidewalks run parallel to streets,
but they also run perpendicular
to streets.

They cross intersections.
They love the park
and move versus cars.
Sidewalks zigzag to Shaula Doyle's apartment.
and descend to the waterfront.

Remember this though: The sidewalk is only
—and always—
parallel to the sky.

Orient yourself.

Light rail travels parallel to future polling places.
The port reclines adjacent to the world.
Students share rooms oblique to world history.
Buildings rise next to buildings at right angles to nightclubs,
with piano chords stirring inside.

Music is written parallel to invocations.

Billie Holiday stands in the hallway, extending her arms
—parallel to what?

Remember: When you're living in a city, you're conducting a seance.

A year in the forest

Anna Hillary

My own fur
Was beautiful, if not much more
Than all the fleeting moments, piled "hi's"
Slaps on the back,
A belly rub with the slippery side.

That's the one I choose, (un)certainly
Heaven opened up, and the shimmering wonder
Cemented into home below.
Floor to ceiling, generations of waste
The house, its walls a confessional en masse,
Holidays exposed for reasons she knows.
Tangled mess wrought clean
By butterfly wings. Silken sorry
I got you in my dreams
Still listening
I'm ready to fight for me.

"A Complete Stillness" a Fine Art Surf Photography Series

Justin Snyder

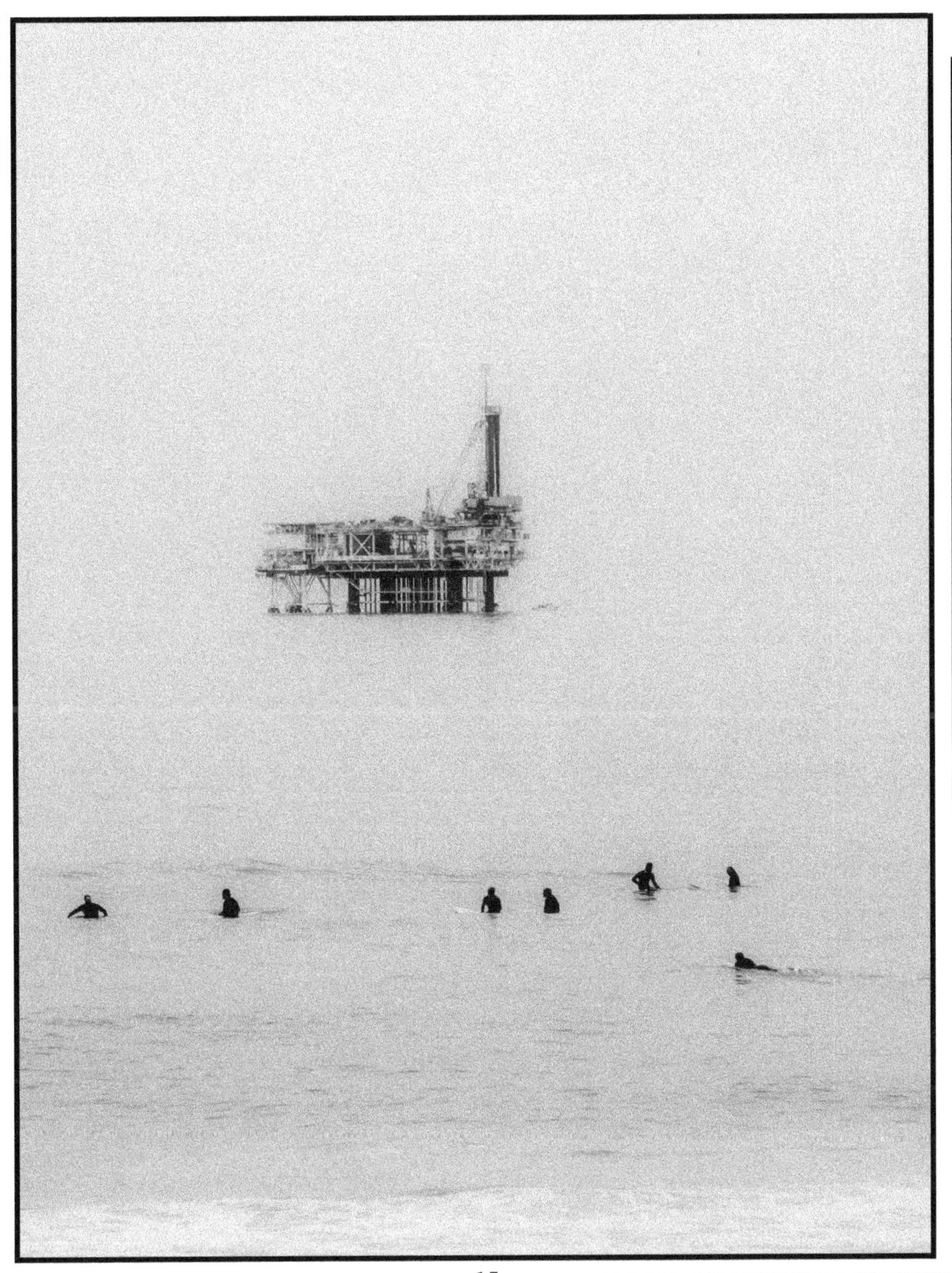

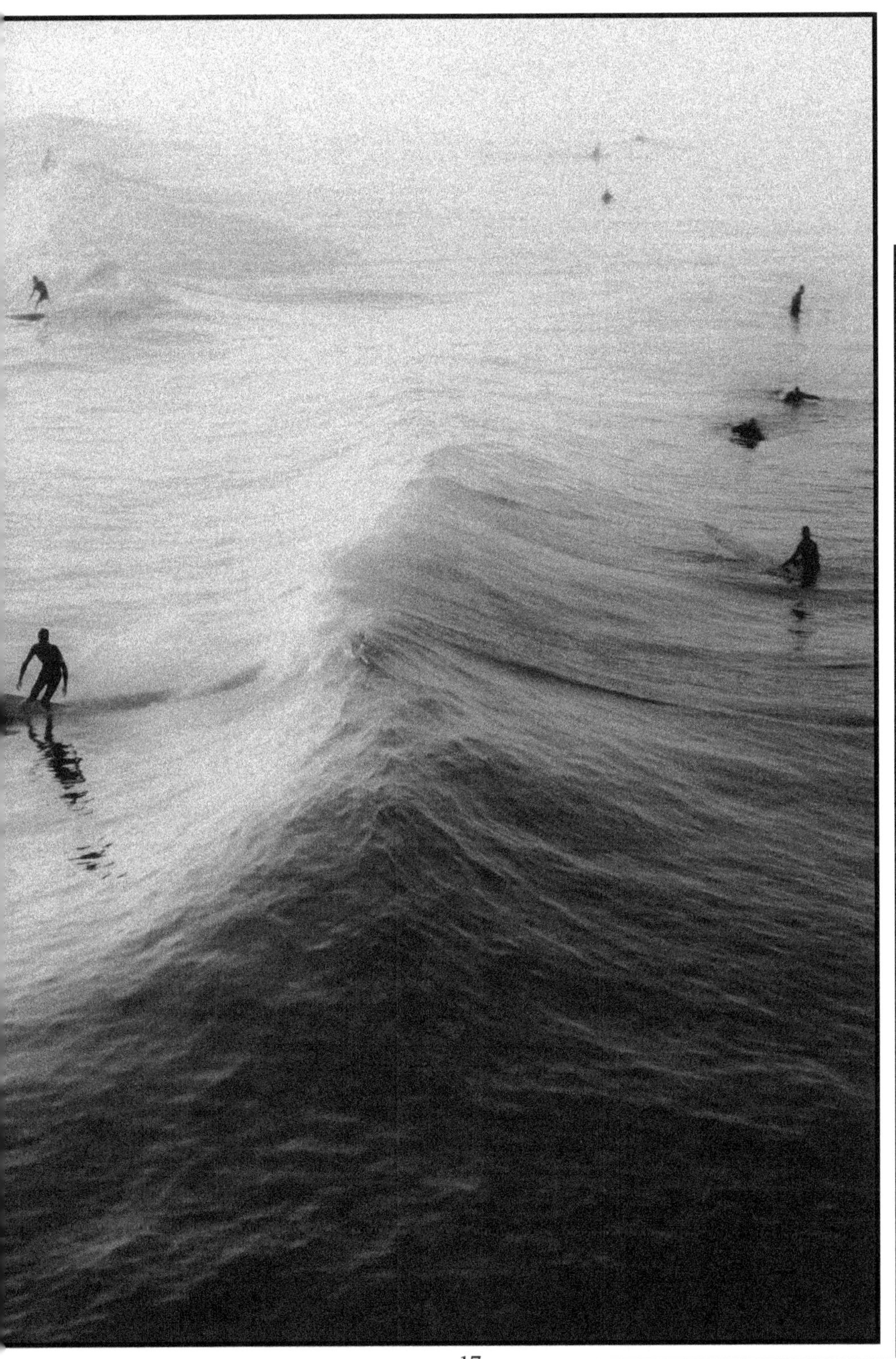

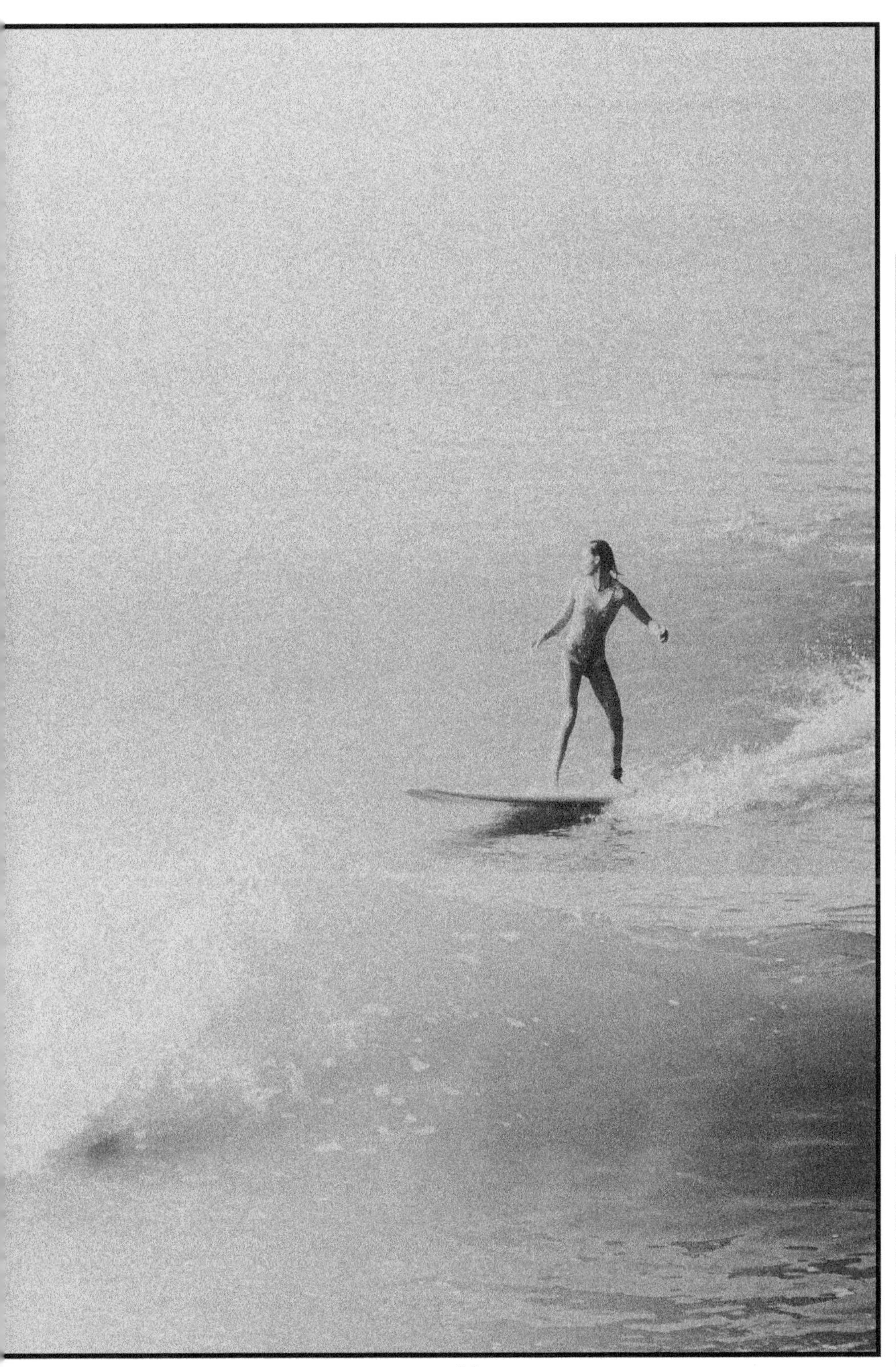

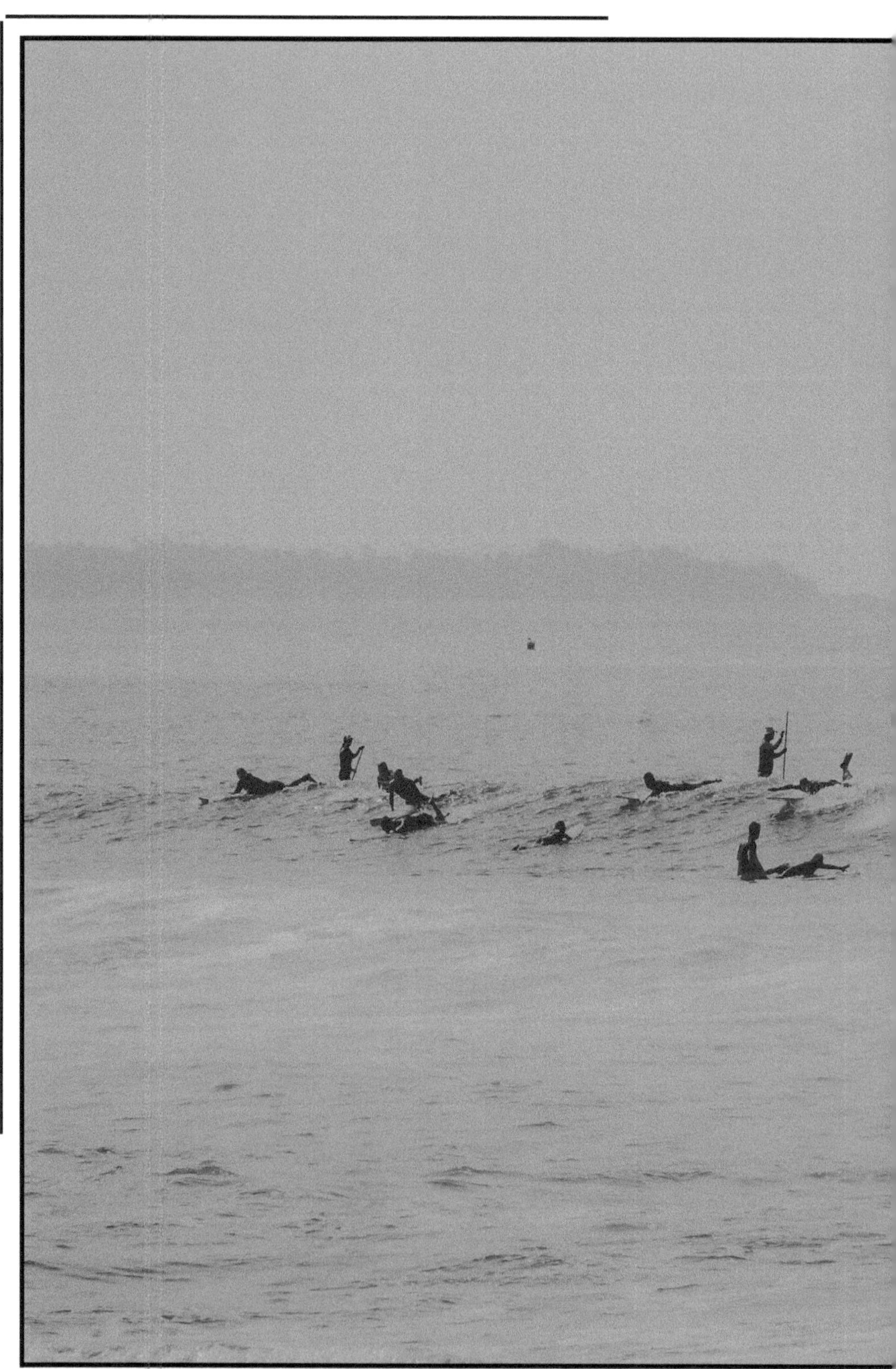

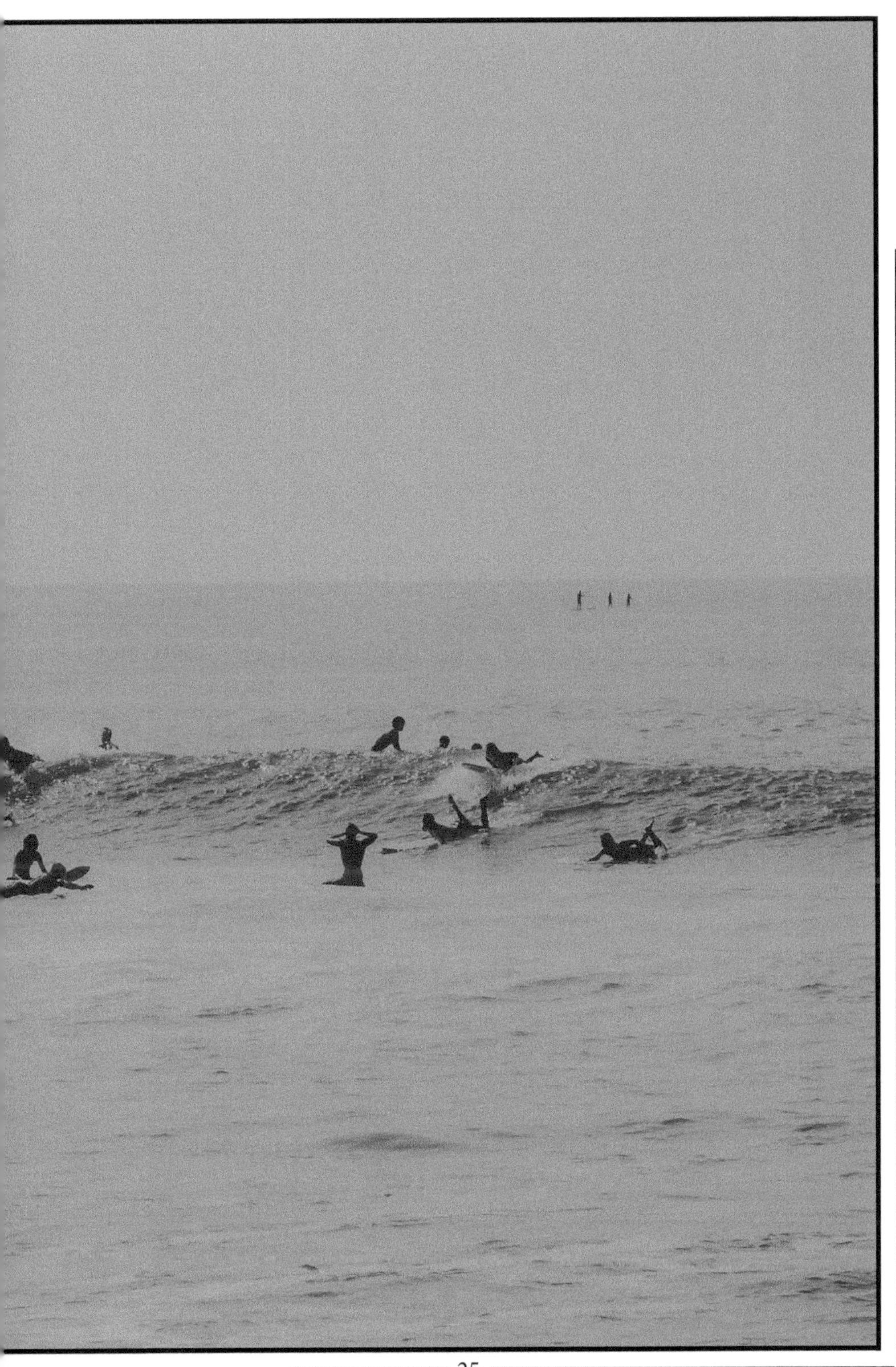

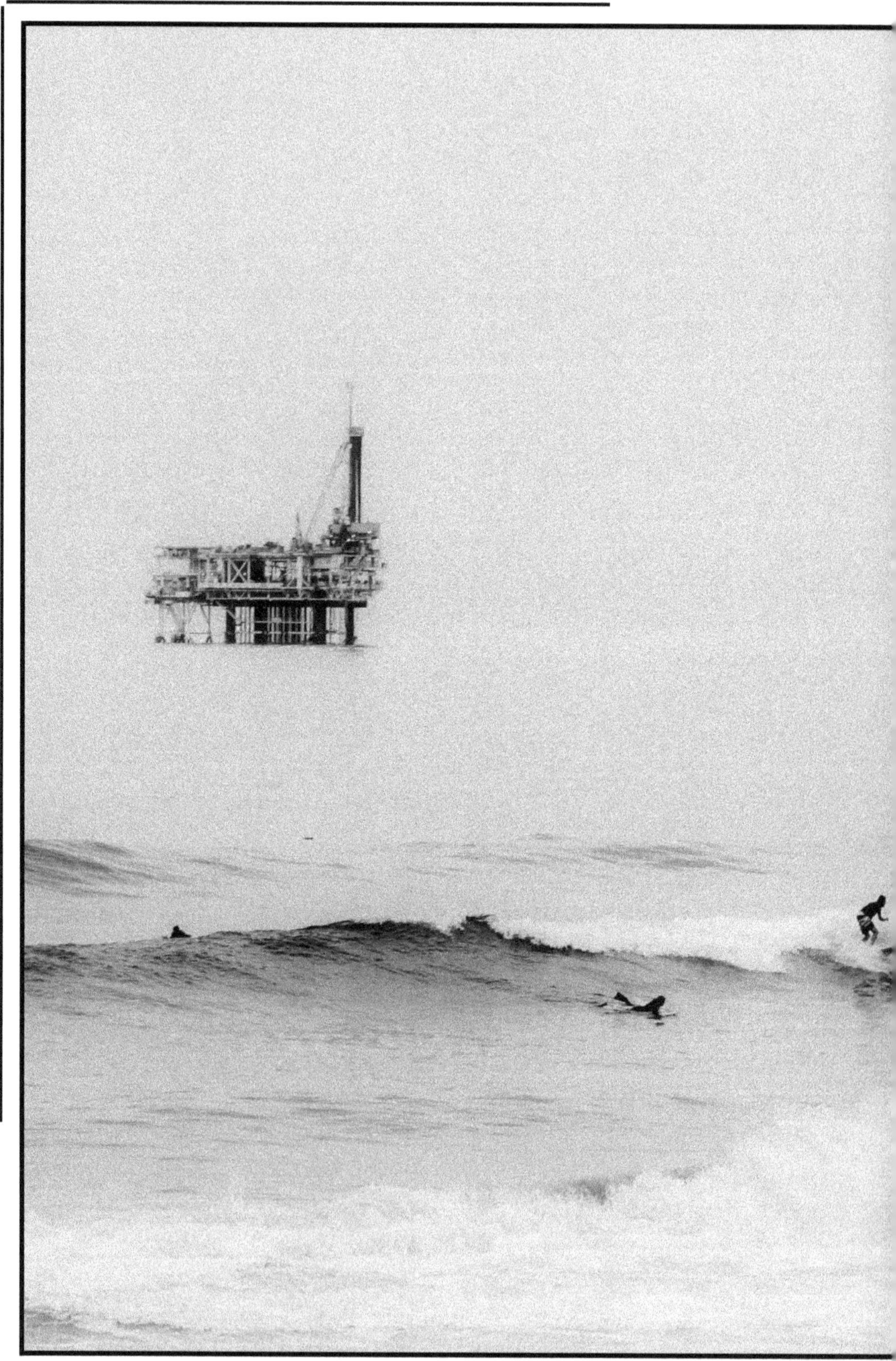

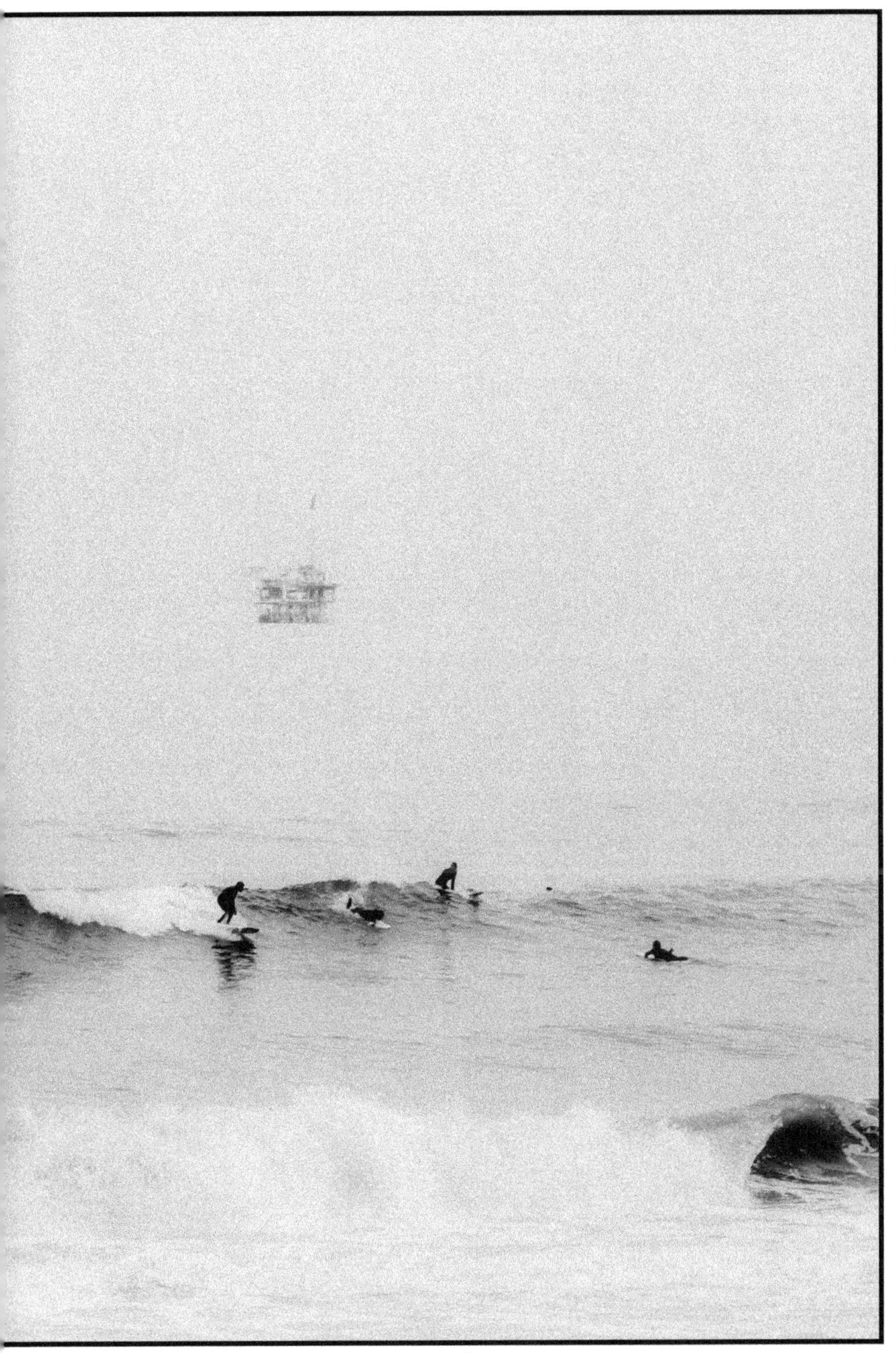

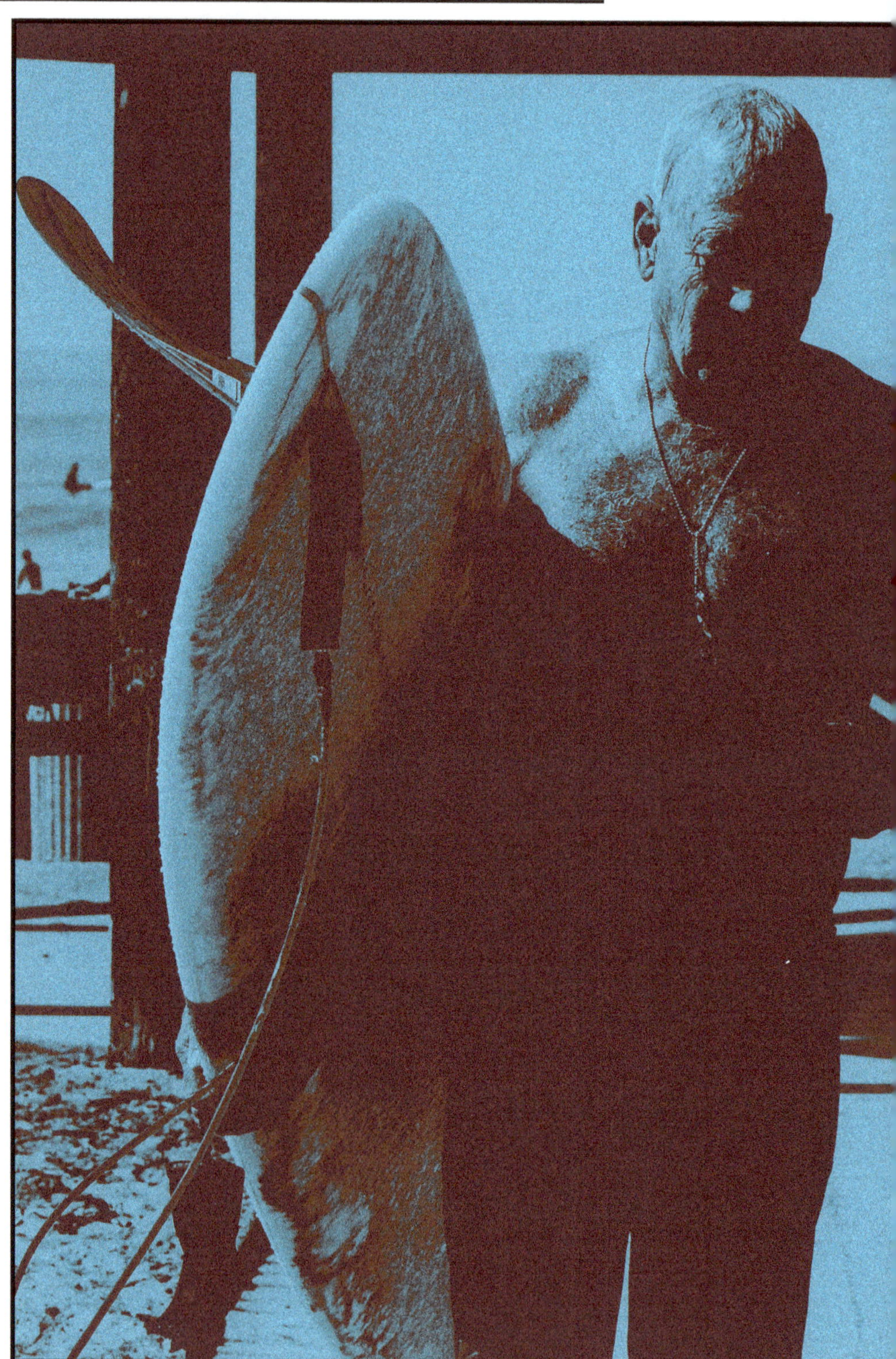

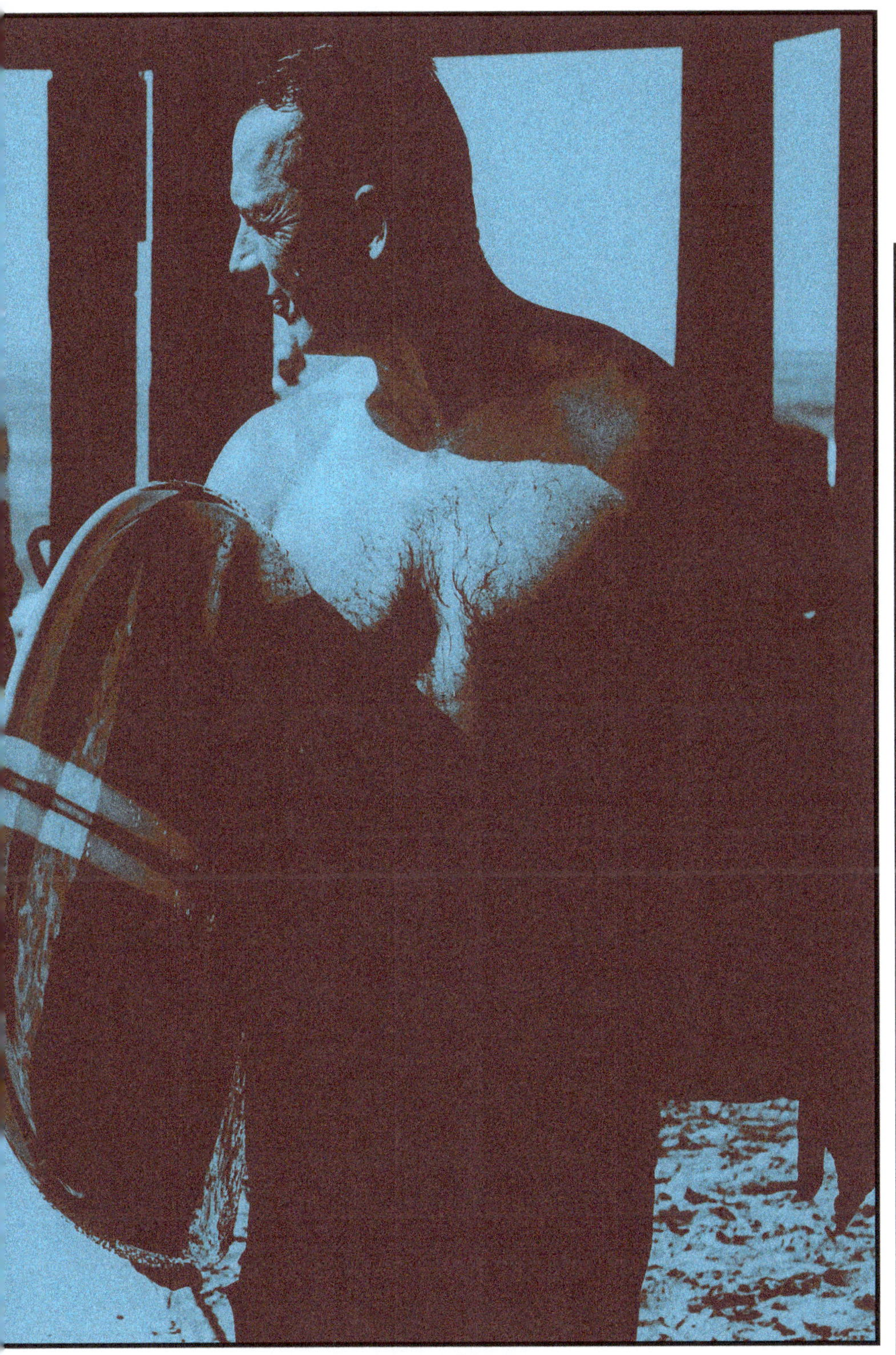

Birds Know

Nancy Klepsch

Even a bird knows

Where to build

How to find food

Who to partner

Birds know

When to take flight

What to bring

Who to sing and dance with

Even birds know

Who is prey

Who is predator

When to break free

Where to fly

Birds know

Headstones

Walter Weinschenk

Pity those headstones by the road:
They languish in the crowded yard;
They guard their dead, stand vigil over them
Like sentries massed in perfect rows
But never do they speak among themselves
Out of fealty to those who lie beneath.

Abandoned, left alone to persevere:
No family left to care for them,
No sons or daughters in the lineage
To lay flowers at their feet
On a Sunday afternoon
Or clear away the weeds;
They are orphans now.

The old grey slab stands alone,
Hidden in the corner:
It leans like some old uncle,
Knees and ankles misaligned,
Features cracked and rearranged,
Waist worn thin, shoulders bent,
Its skin grown rough and pale,
The name no longer legible;
Chiseled words and numbers
Recede like memories,
Lost in the pyre of age,
And forgotten are the dates
That once were clearly etched
Upon the front like a person's face
That grew tired and absurd
In the months before he died,
A face that mocked the face
That he once wore
When he was young
And ruled the world,
Long before he understood
That he, in time, would die.

There will come a day
When the very last man
Will leap across a gravel patch

Where once a headstone stood,
Planted so long ago
By a broken, arrogant few
To demark the life of one they loved
For the rest of time to come
But whose name will be lost before too long;
And when that runner has run his race,
No one will be left to know of humankind itself,
No one to know that men and women
Walked the ground and lived their lives;
New seas will rise and drown the earth
And will flood the yard,
And all those orphan stones
And all those bones and the ground itself
Will wash away, and fish will swim
Where rows of headstones stood;
But, even so, one can't deny that, yesterday,
There lived a man who was once alive
And when he lived, his life was real:
A headstone testifies that he existed,
Proclaims the truth of the dream
That was his life, and defines
His soul in space and time
And, for today, at least,
Holds vigil over him.

Floating

Margo Griffin

Heavy rain keeps coming, never ceasing,
flooding almost empty streets.
I see the leaves, orange straws and debris,
floating down toward the riverbank.

I make myself small, no larger than a pebble,
shrinking and fitting on a boat made of leaf.
I am floating, twisting and turning in a stream,
safe in the crevice between sidewalk and street.

I glide down the cool rain's river path,
sailing swiftly to my watery escape.
I am sent down a slip made of grass and puddle,
launched into the river, set adrift by the wind.

I drift downstream in my journey to open sea,
searching for a home free from pain.
I remain elated and buoyant, kept afloat,
by the promise of an ocean home meant for me.

NOT CONCEPTUAL: LIFE

Catherine Lieser

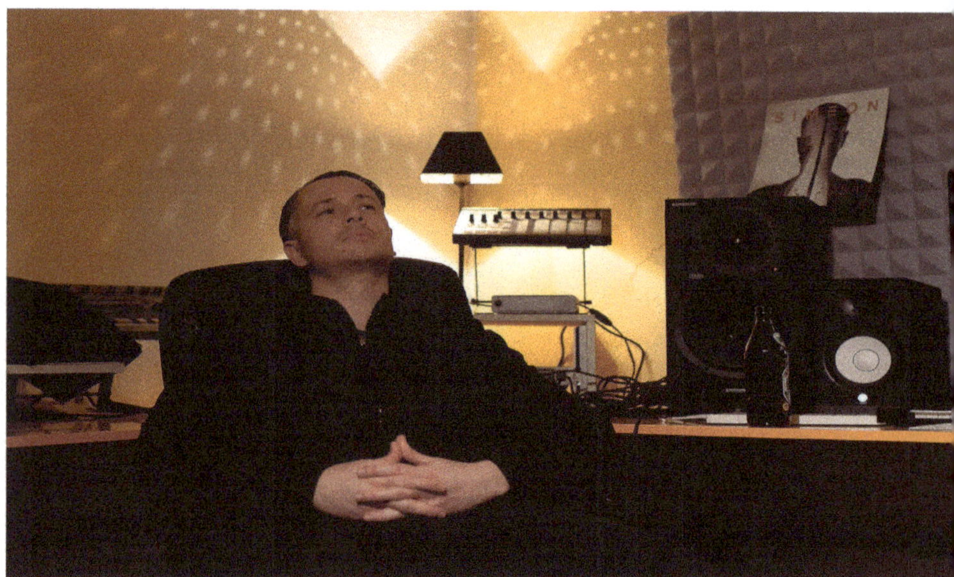

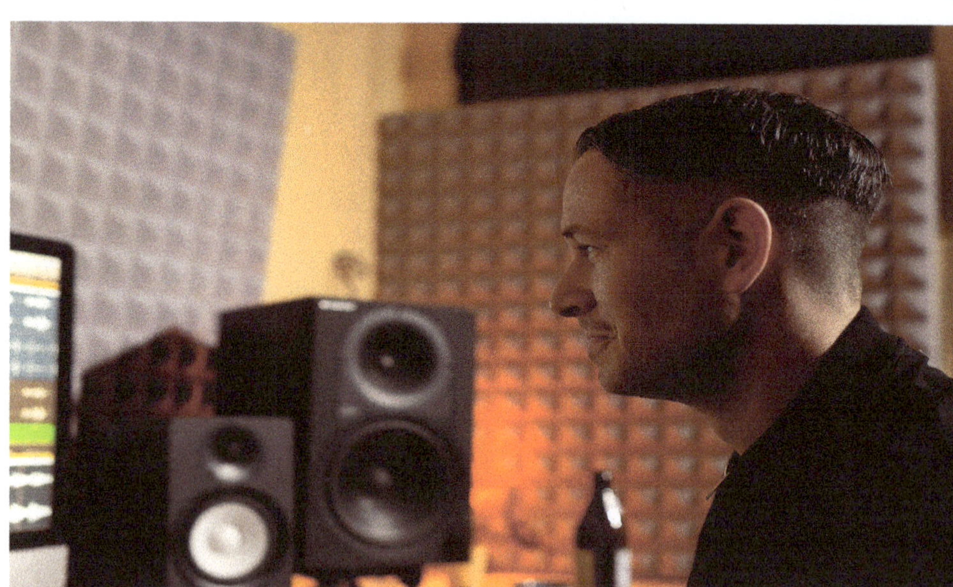

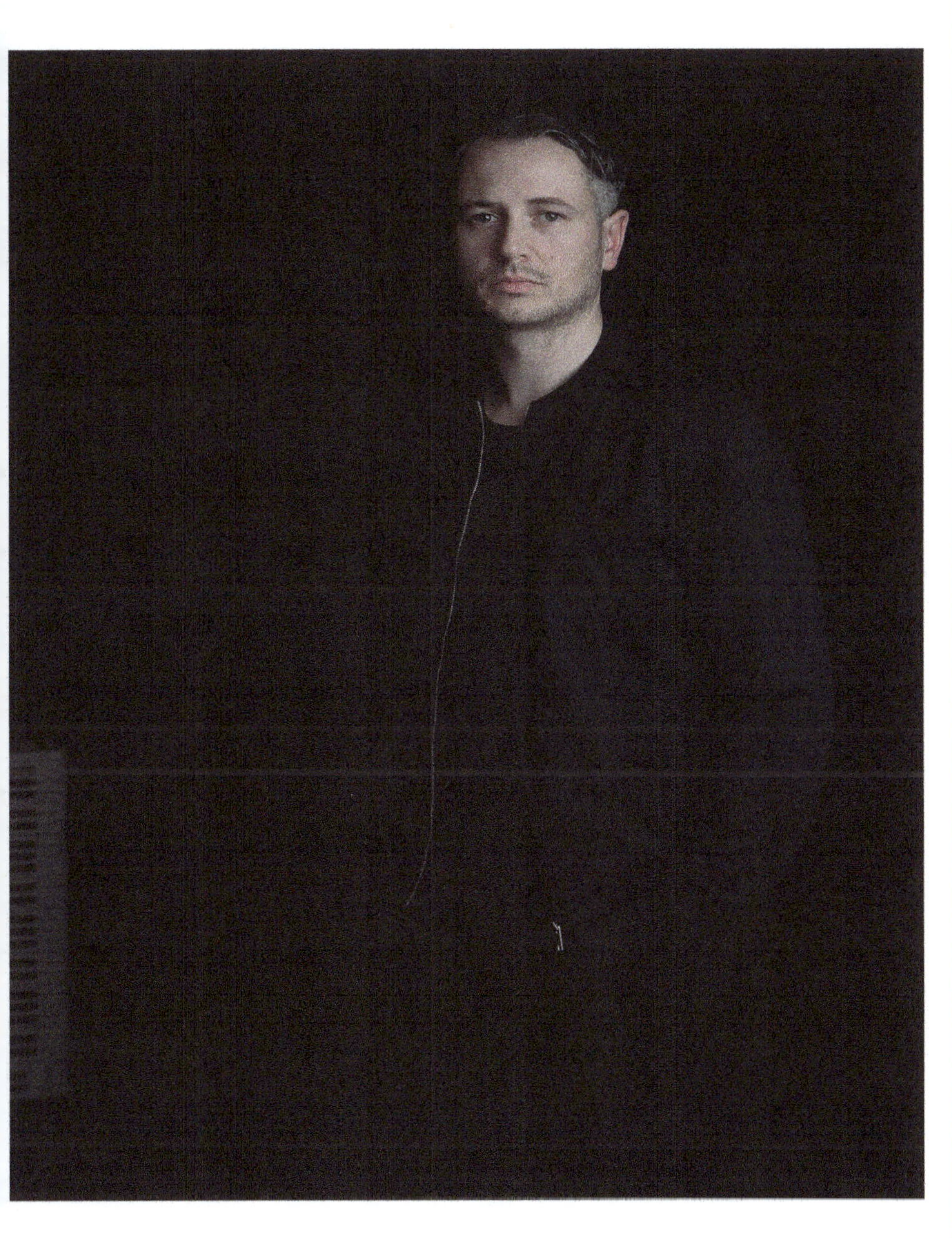

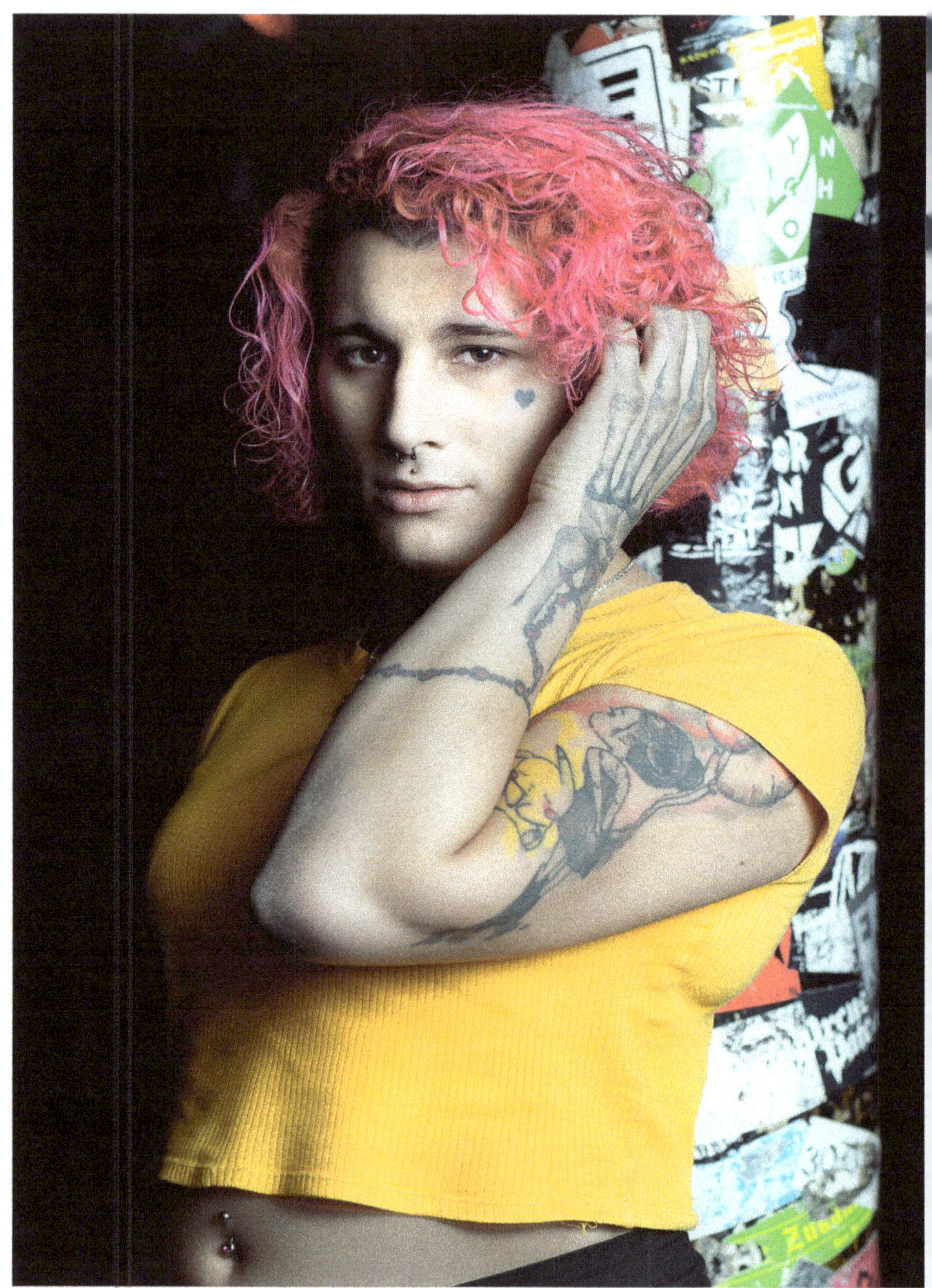

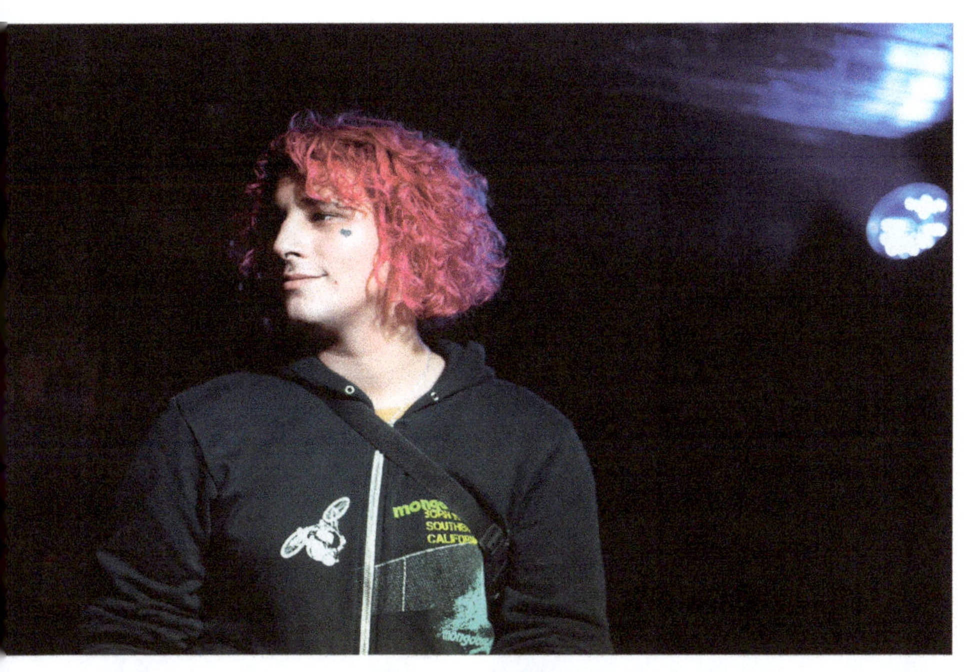

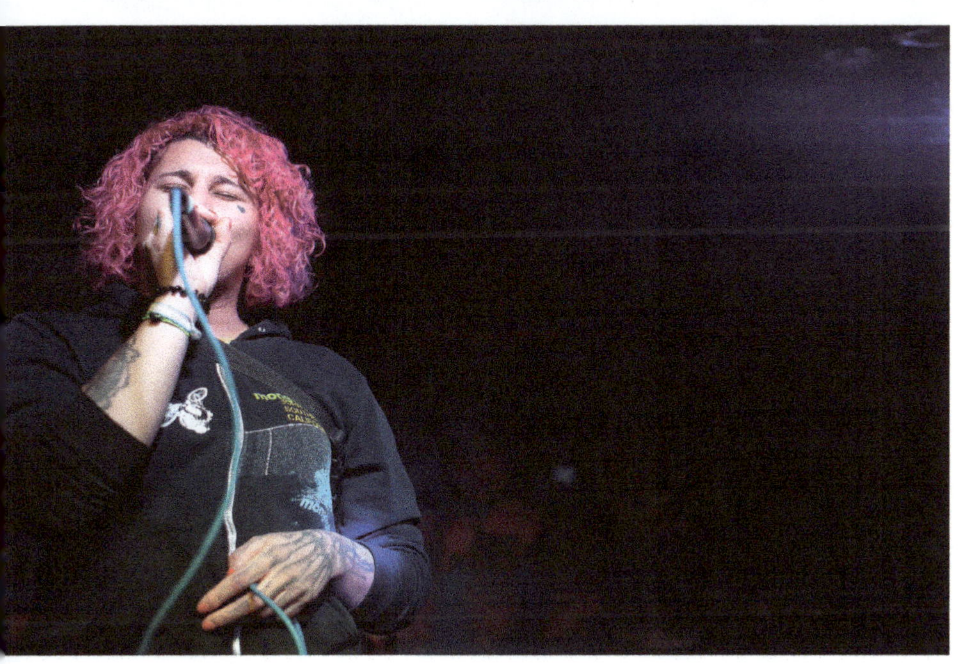

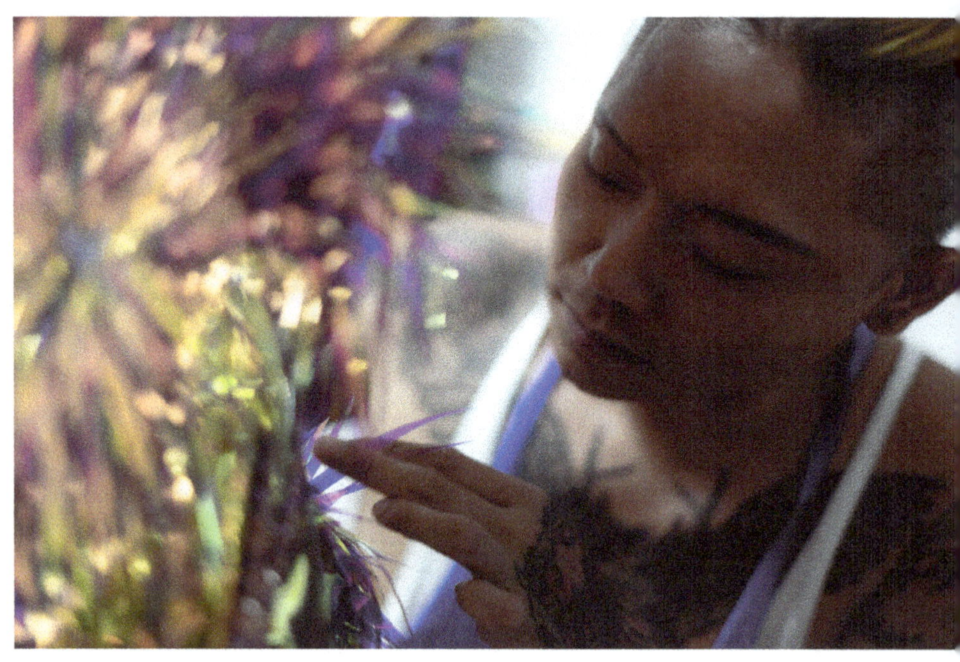

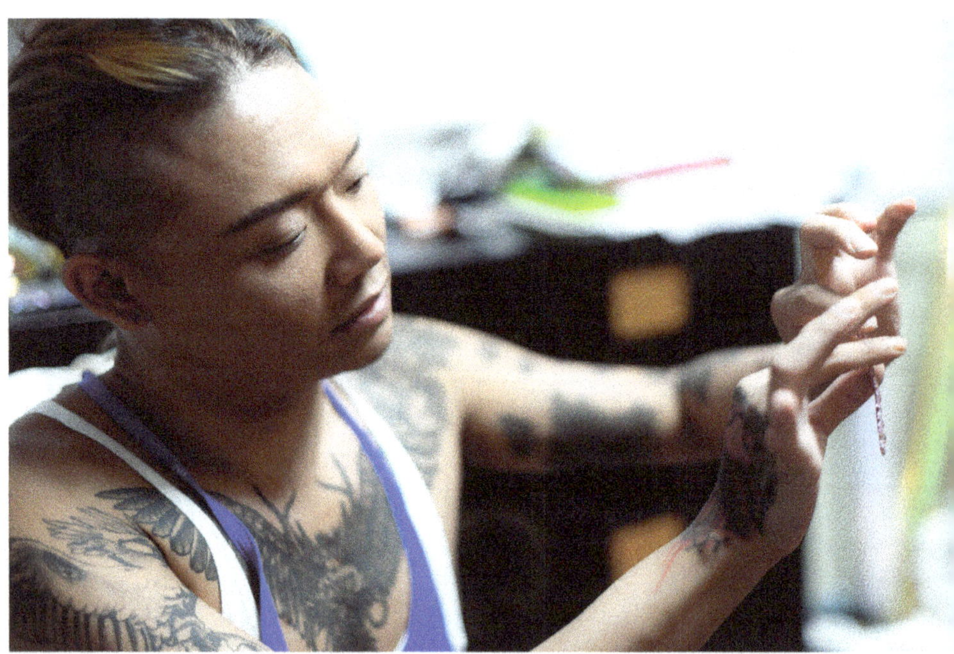

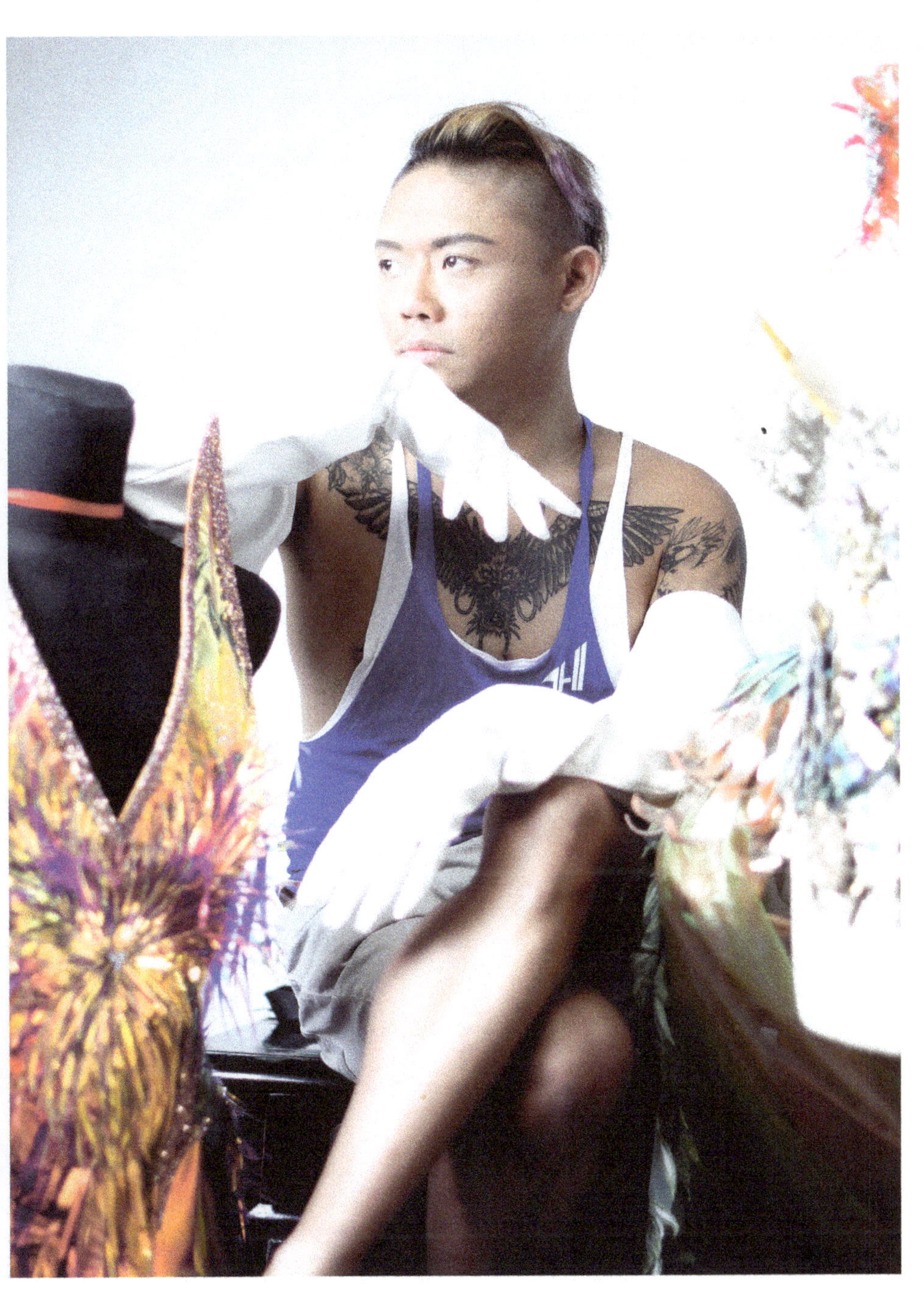

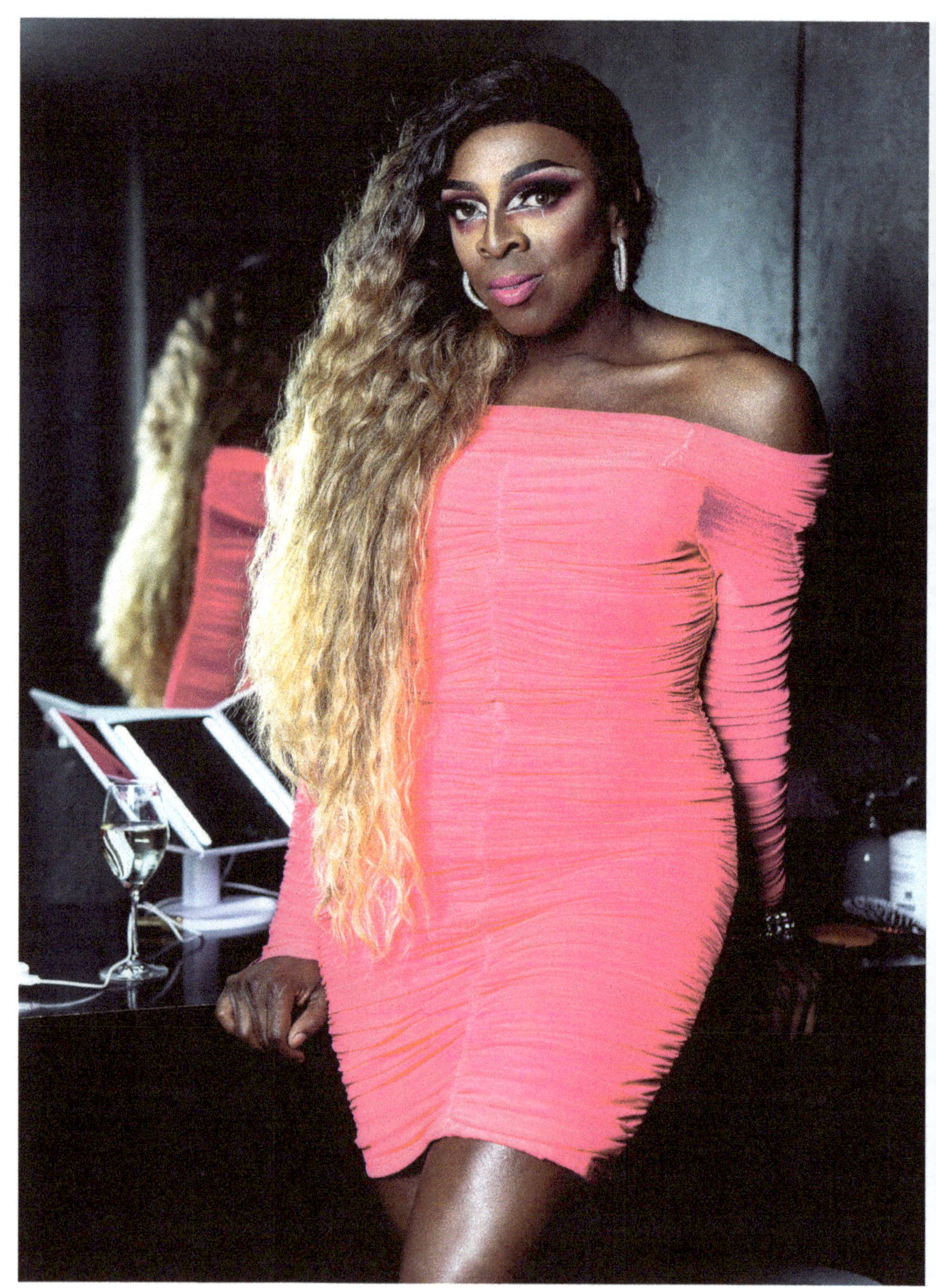

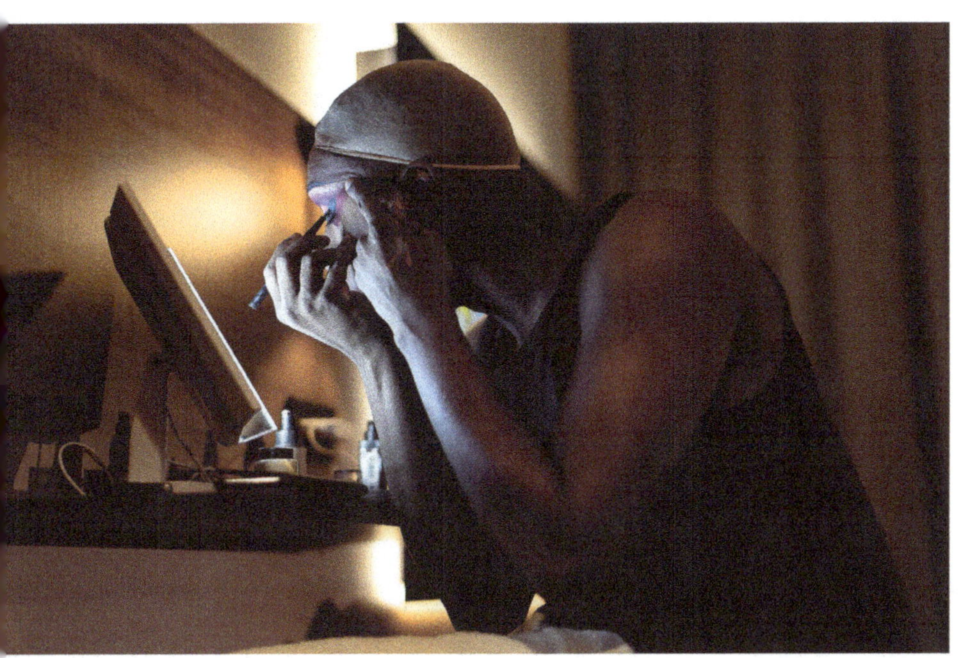

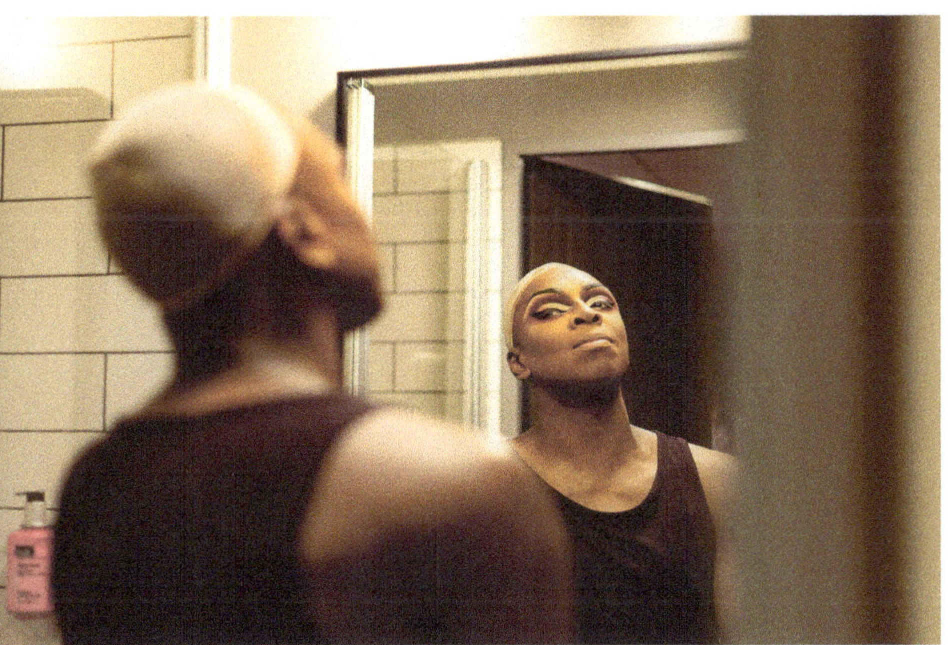

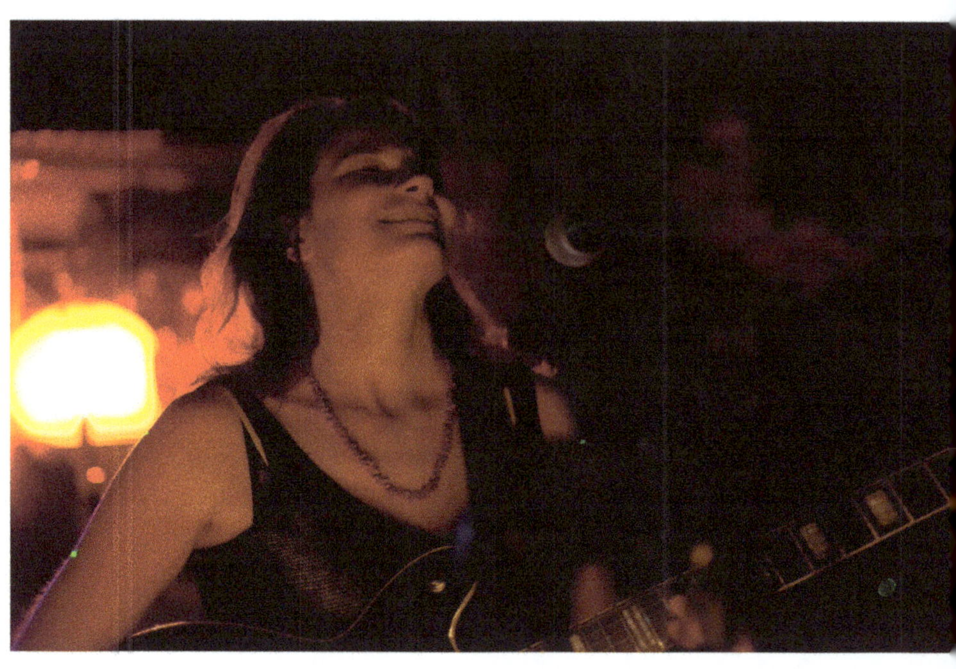

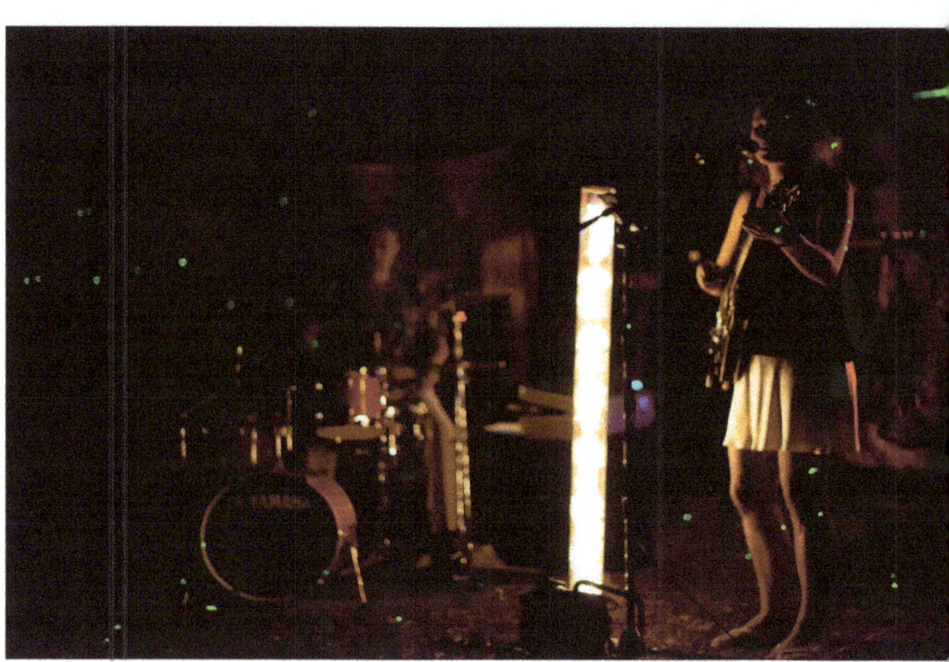

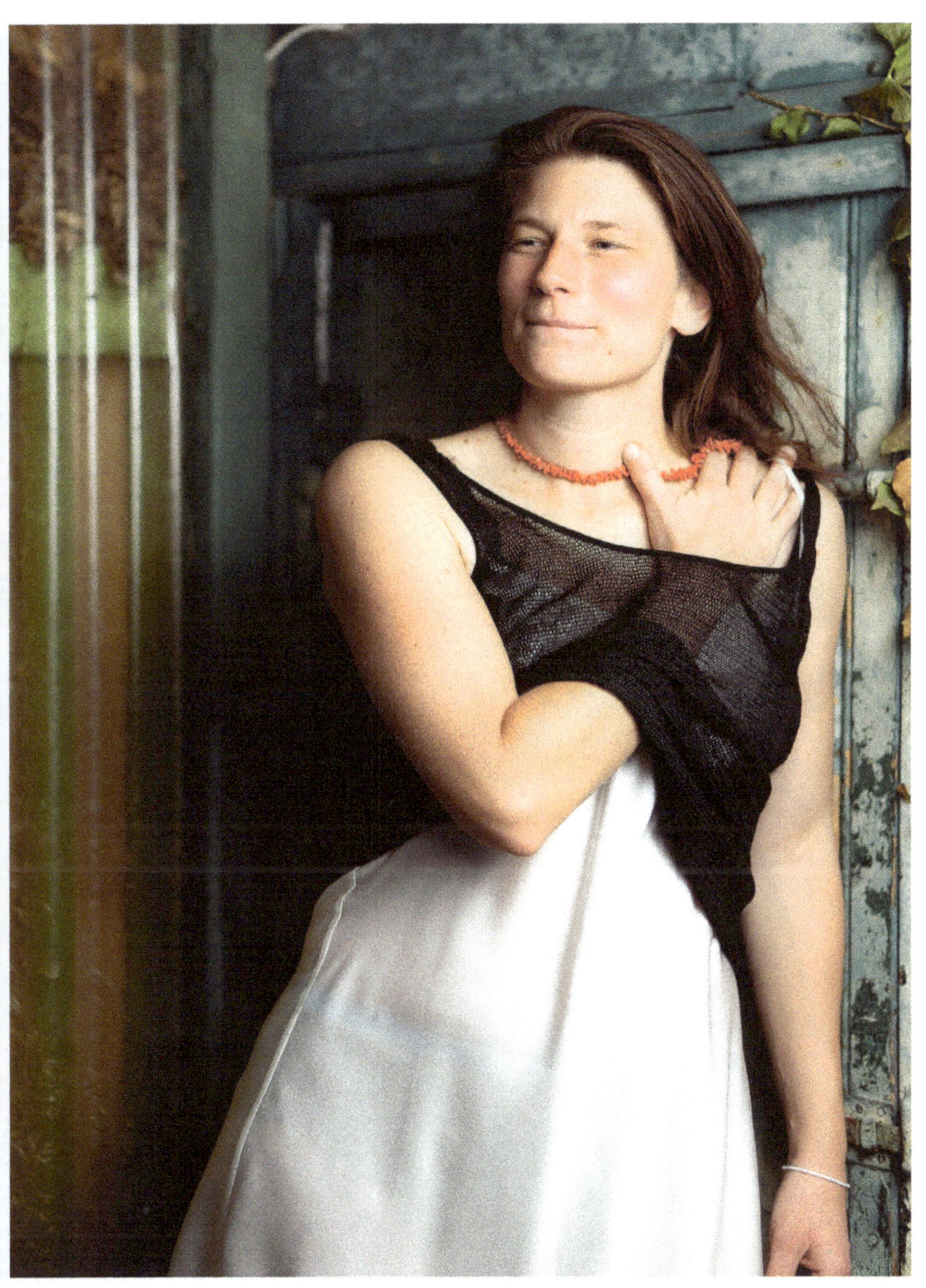

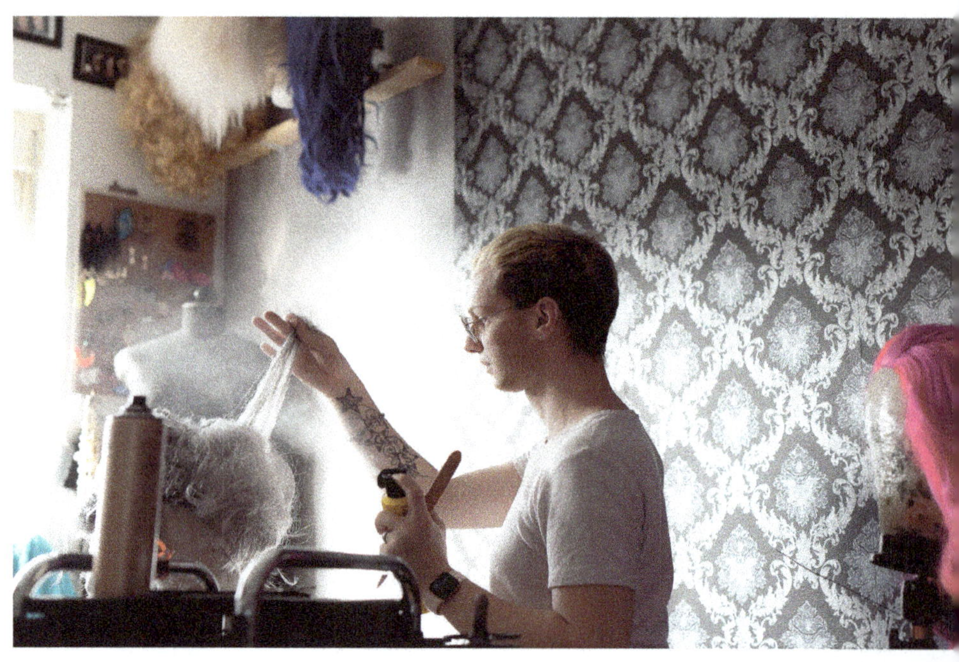

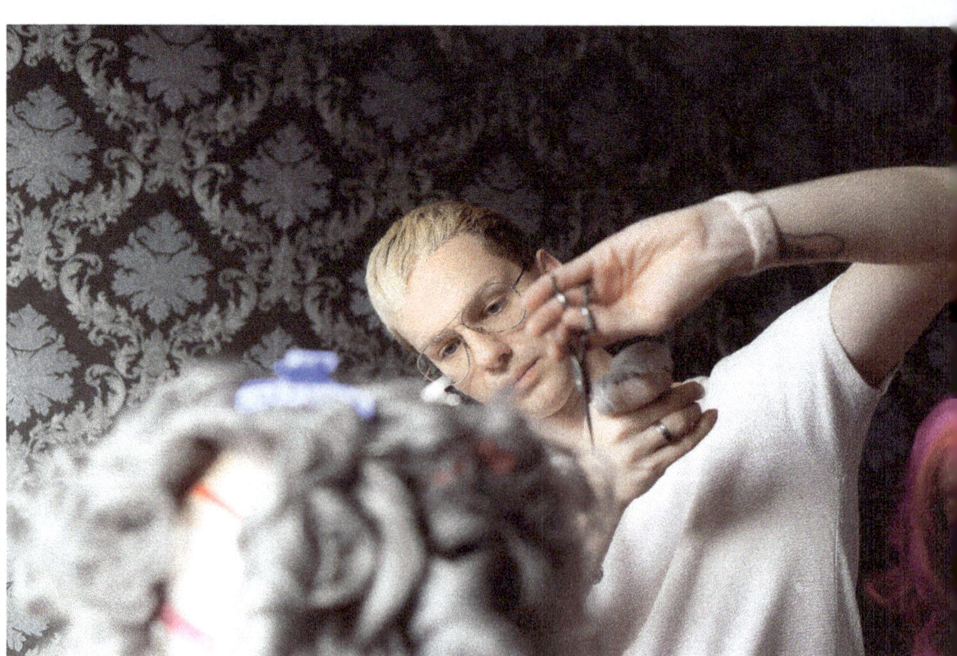

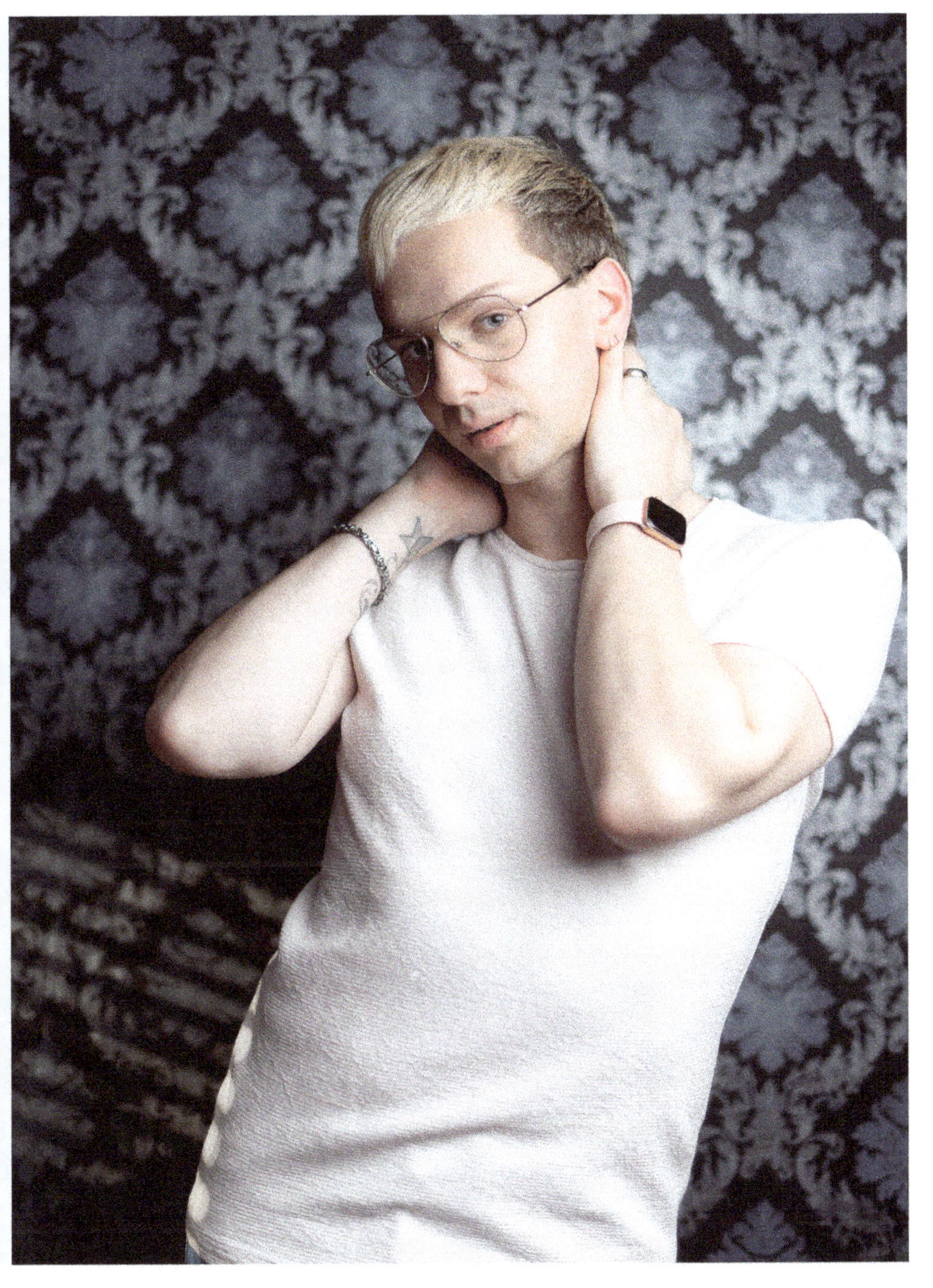

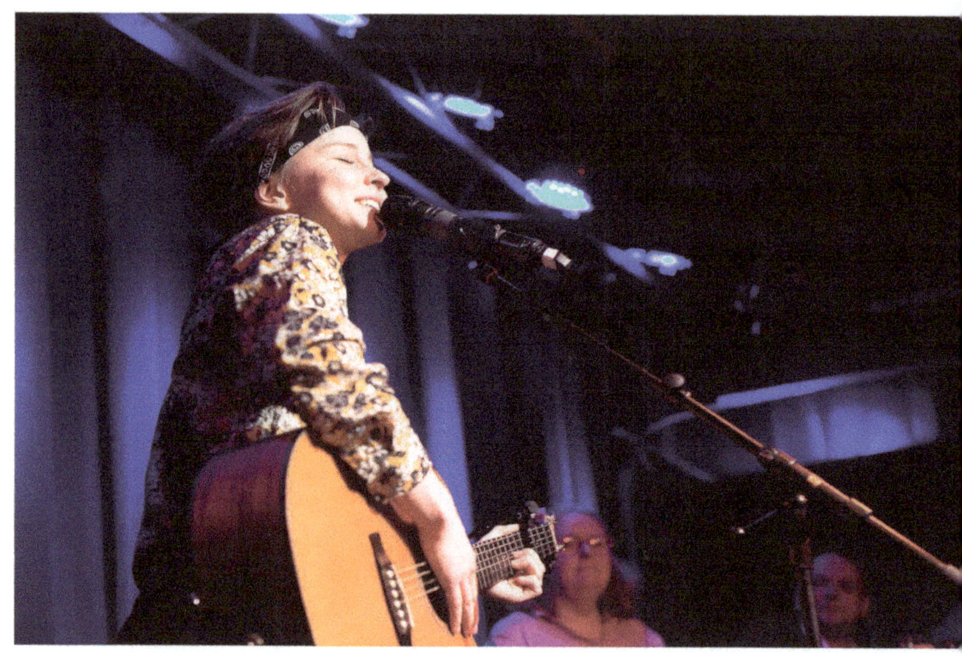

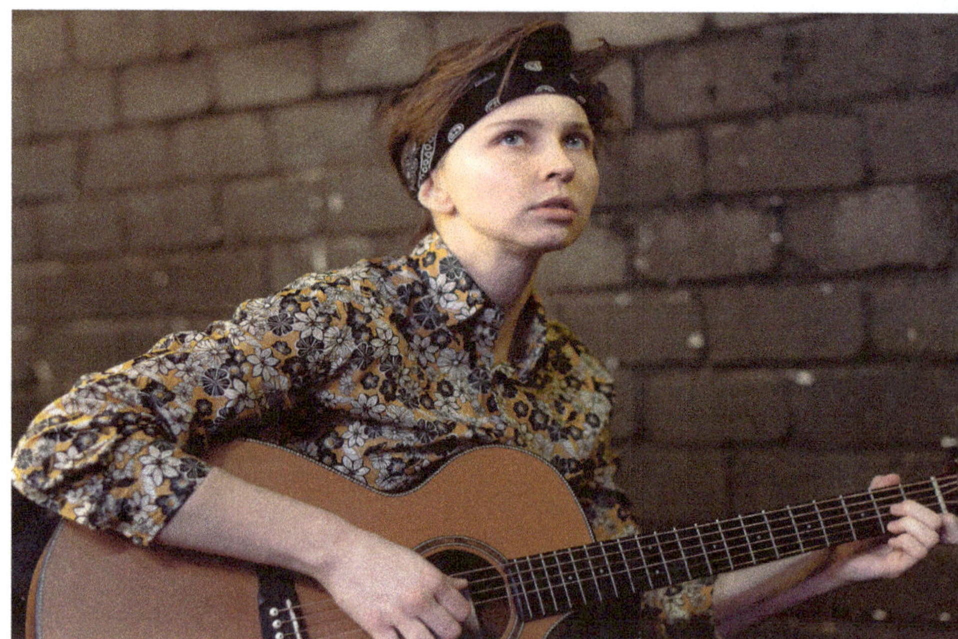

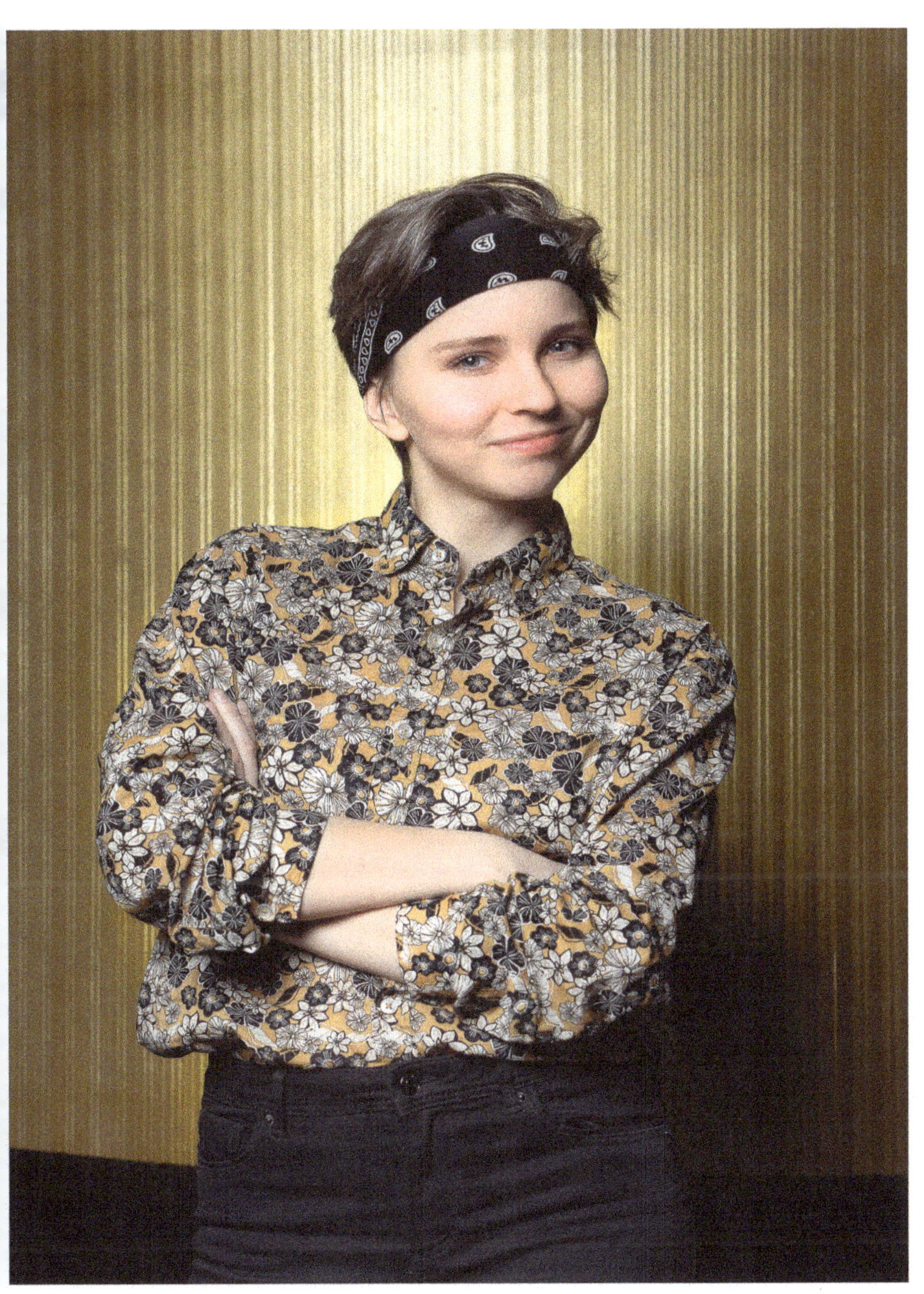

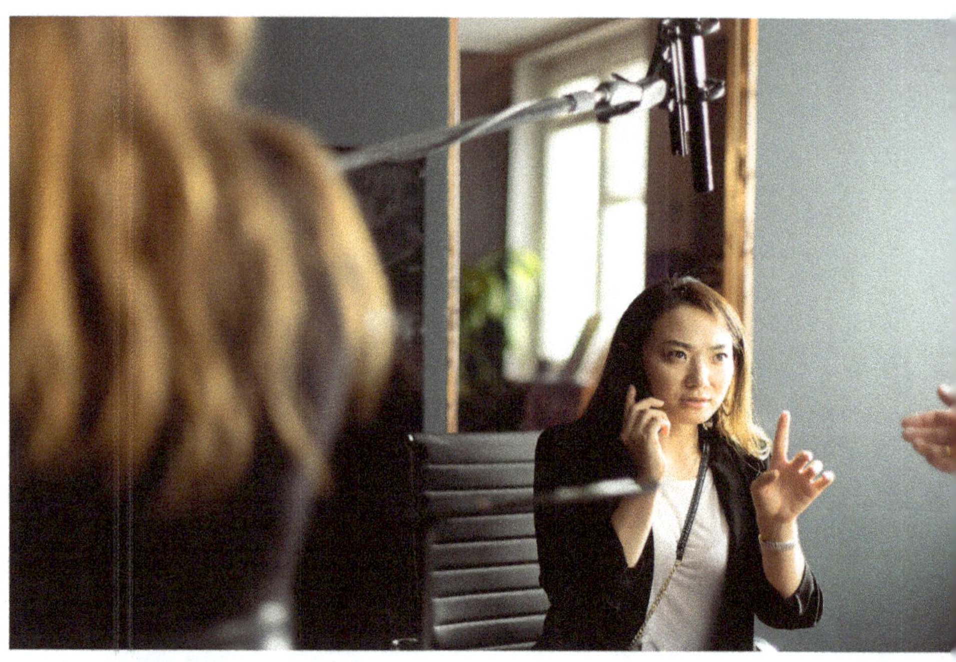

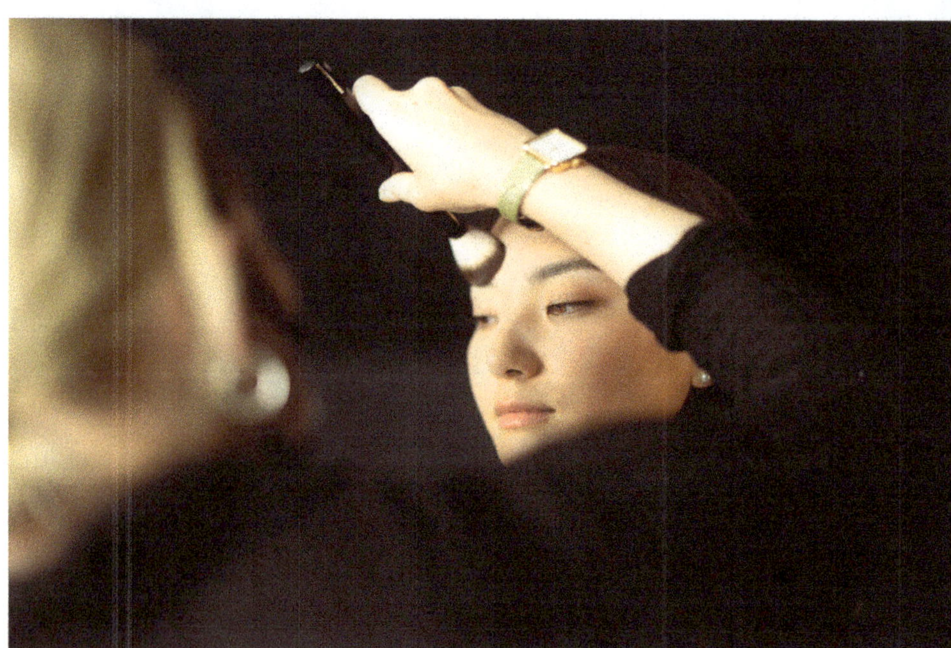

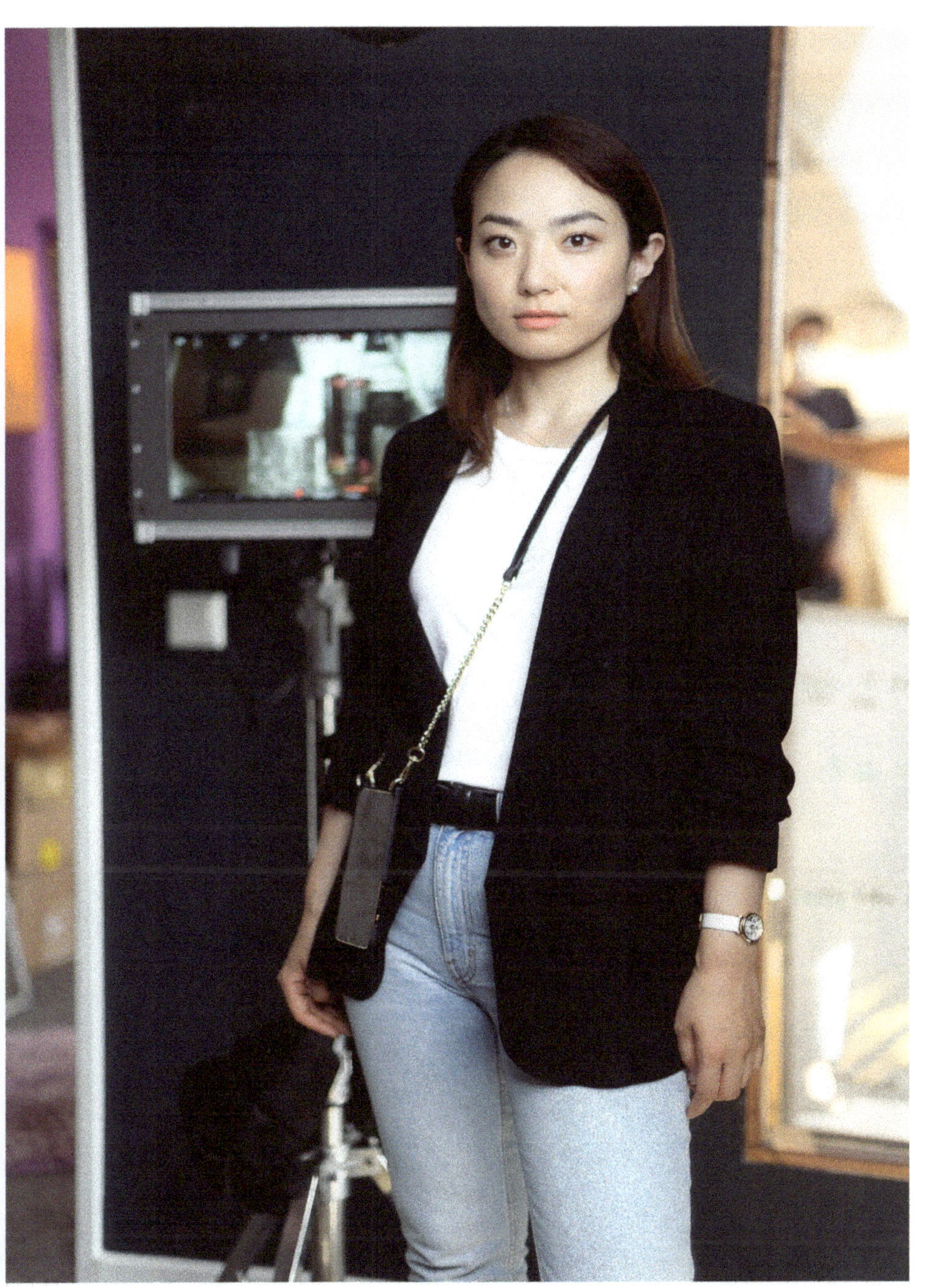

Art of GJ Gillespie

GJ Gillespie

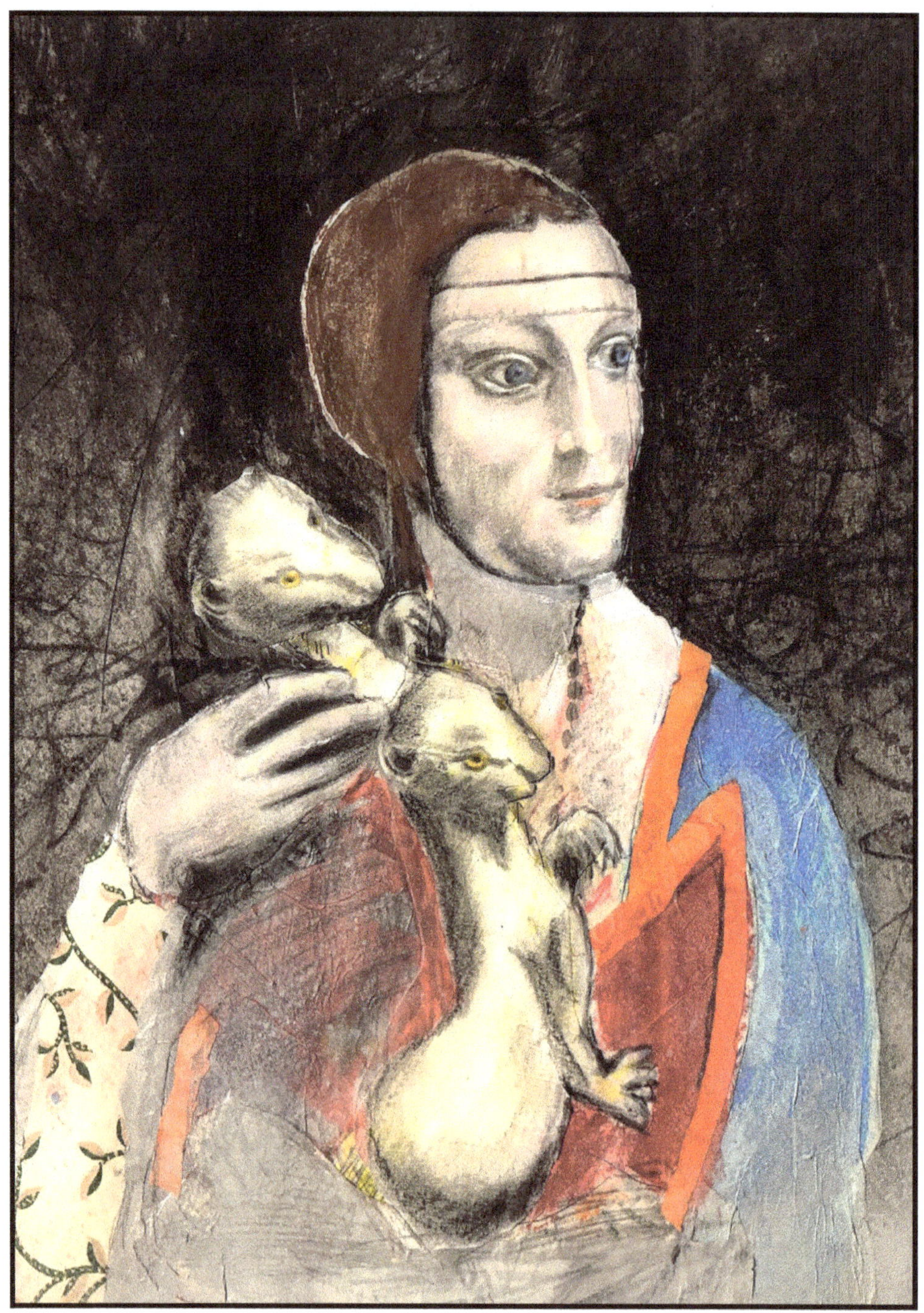

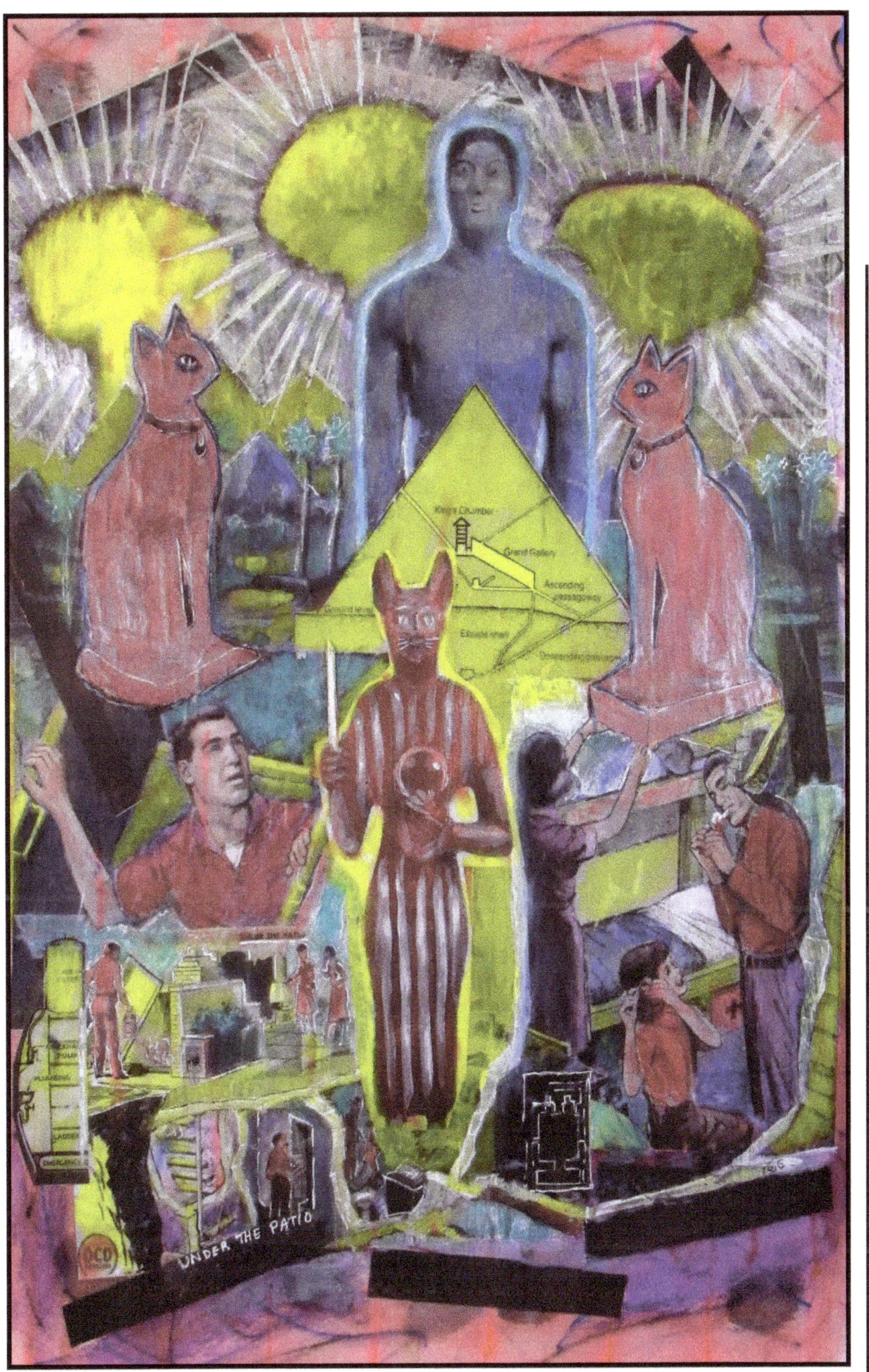
King's Chamber
Grand Gallery
Ascending passageway
Ground level
Escape shaft
Descending passageway
UNDER THE PATIO
OCD
PLUMBING
LADDER

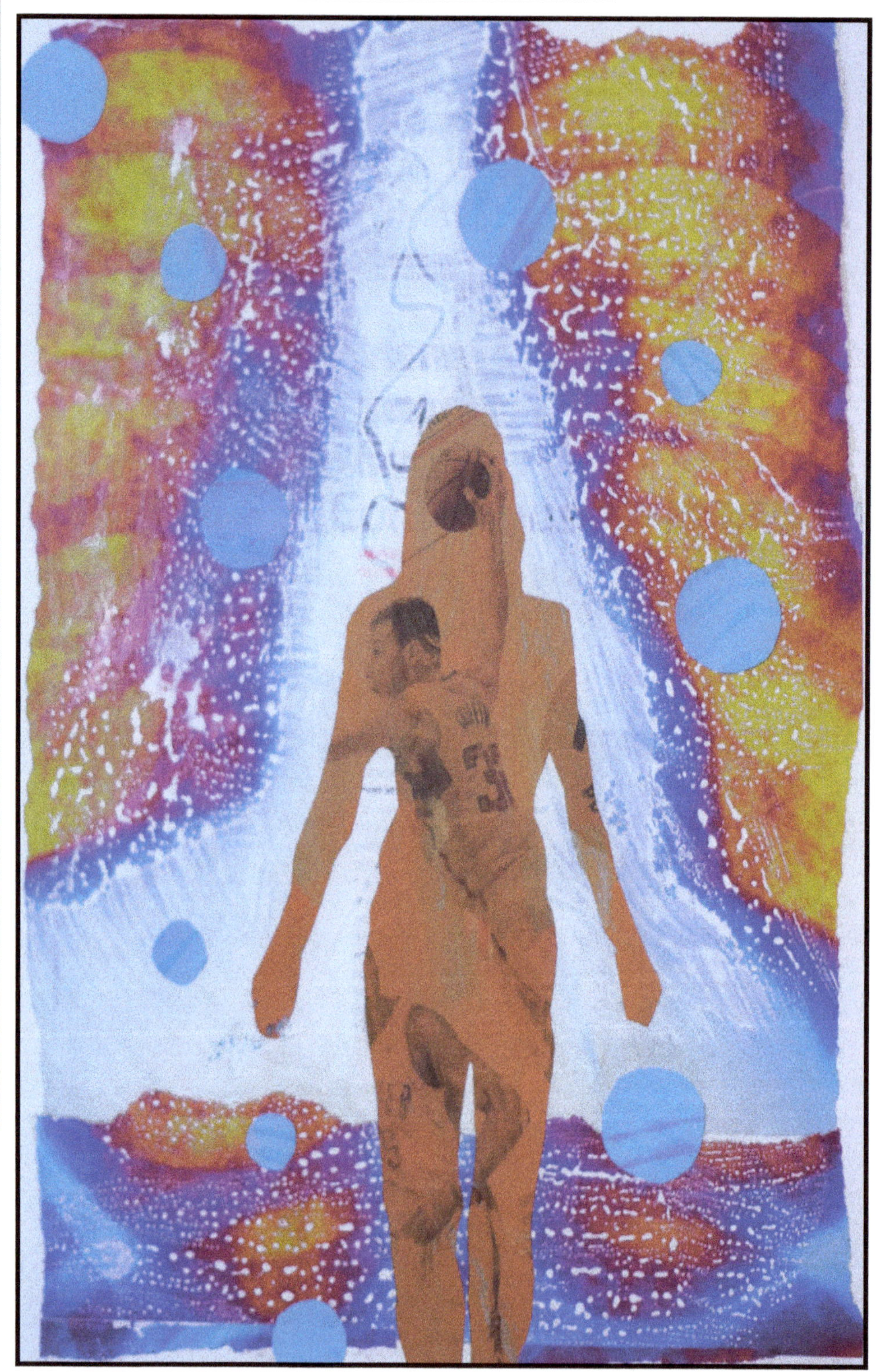

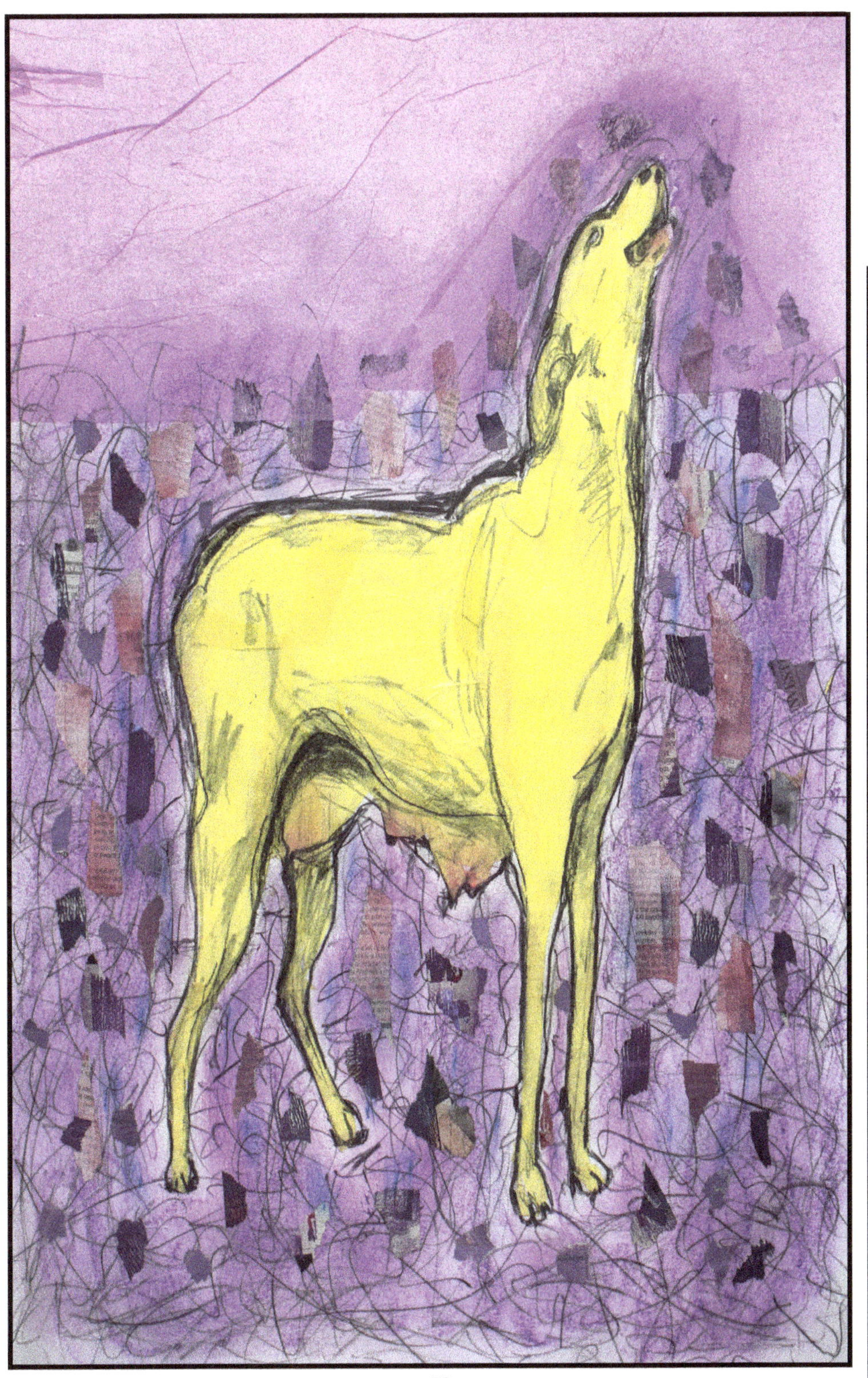

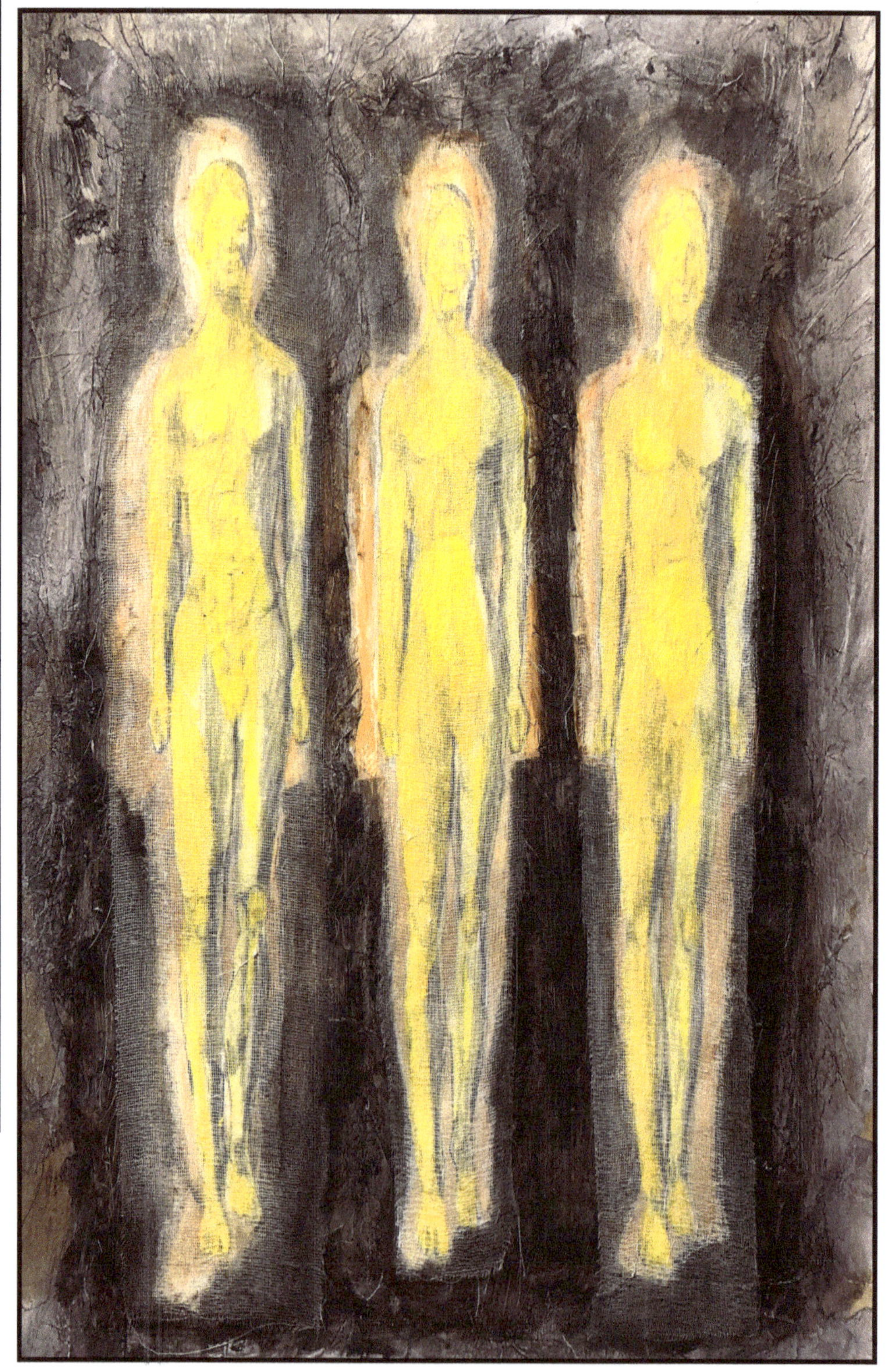

IN NINETEEN WHATEVER

Greg Sendi

They are not lunatics, hypochondriacs, or frenetics; but they have a mixture of all these kinds of diseases, which, injuring their minds, cause them to become more ravenous than starving dogs, and make them so hungry for human flesh, that they fall on women and children, even on men, like actual werewolves, and devour them rapaciously.

Relations des Jésuites de la Nouvelle-France (1661)

In nineteen whatever my brothers and I
bought a derelict place built from PVC, pine logs,

some sheetrock and hollow core doors in a recluse
scrub maple stand deep in the Kingdom of Dum.

Look, don't tell me *it's just how things roll in that part
of the mitten*. I don't mean homespun *local color*,

okay? I mean Odic rune dirtbags and methmouthed
faux-butternut shitjacks at every gas pump and

degenerate bumblecunts armed like they work for El
Chapo streaming RPG vids from the woods

and the warped and malignant ex-mayor of Fuckville
who wants (not to over-finesse the point)

camps.

Whenever it was, (say the baby was one
so call it ninety-eight or I think, working back

from the November bonechill the first visit up
on that soupyellow night—there were turkeys out front,

plump with beechnuts and bugs, a whole rafter, so-called
for the roof timbers they would hang from as feast meat—

but, listen, the point is not wildfowl or which
goddamned year, though, for probity's sake, let's just say,

ninety-nine?—since as fathomed the watchful Odawa,
years are inconsequential except to mark famine,

who bequeathed requital to us who came after,
the cannibal Wendigo, bringer of civil

collapse—

and the end of the ways we could hold like to like,
before particleboard and shit plywood and all

the miasmic offgasing formaldehyde resins that
pickled what's left of the upright bluewater

republic, whole hamlets and townships now loopy
and fuddled with kuru in humanflesh frenzies

to signal starvations their broke-brained, dysphasic,
fat famisher-god says they suffer with him

for eternity. Listen, I'm not here to fuss
like some wobbly collegetown sniffy—forearms

are breaching the surface at Antrim and Skegmog
The Rubicon loamsands aren't holding the

corpse.

New Summerfield, 1986

Biff Rushton

The martins would clamour before daylight,
a chant d'amour, draped purple with morning.
I have never forgotten
how their songs drew love across the mirrored
palm of the lake,
and how they fought for their blood
(a war to the knife)
blue/black feathers floating on water

Ketamine Dreams

Zephyr Z

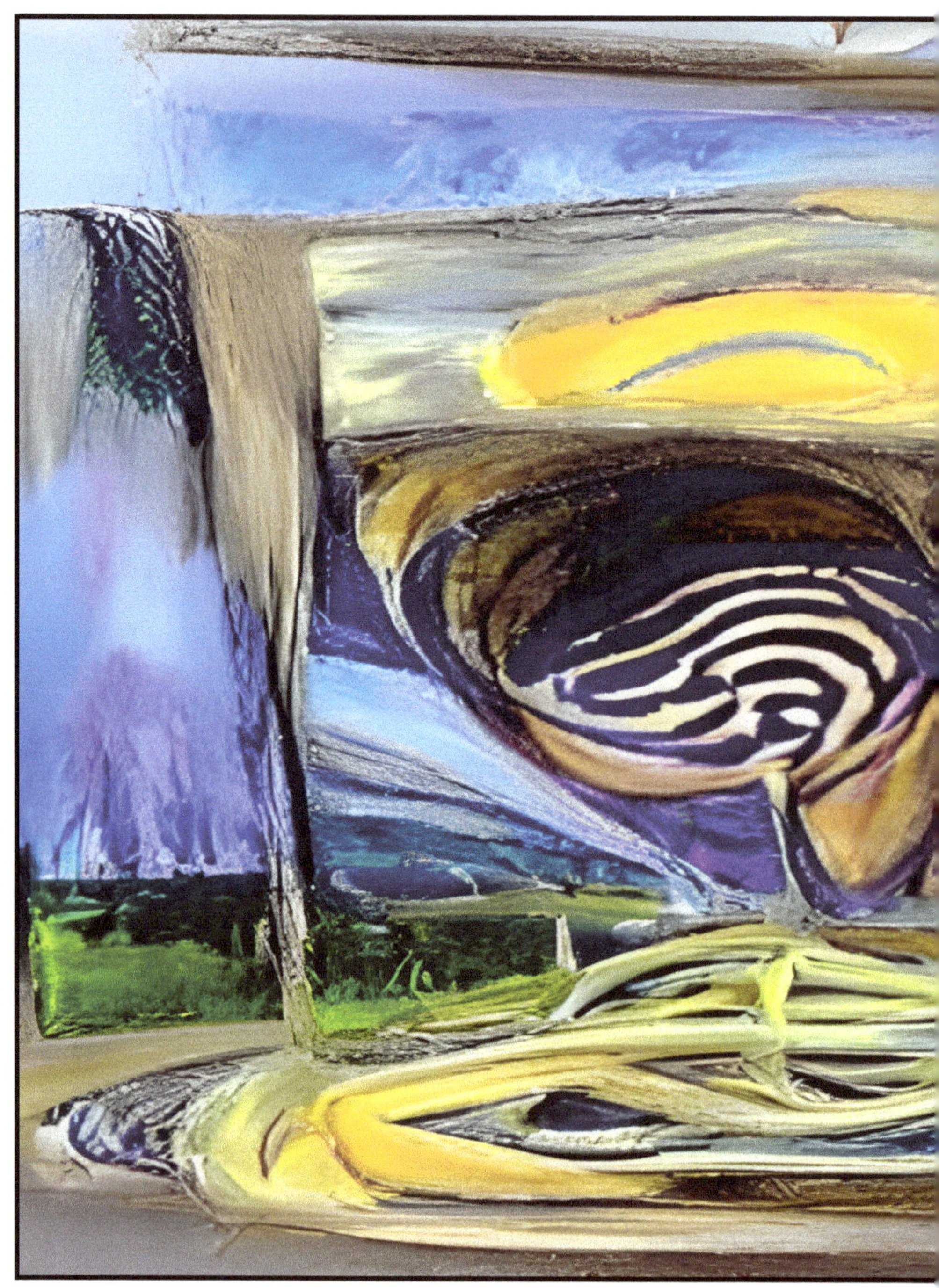

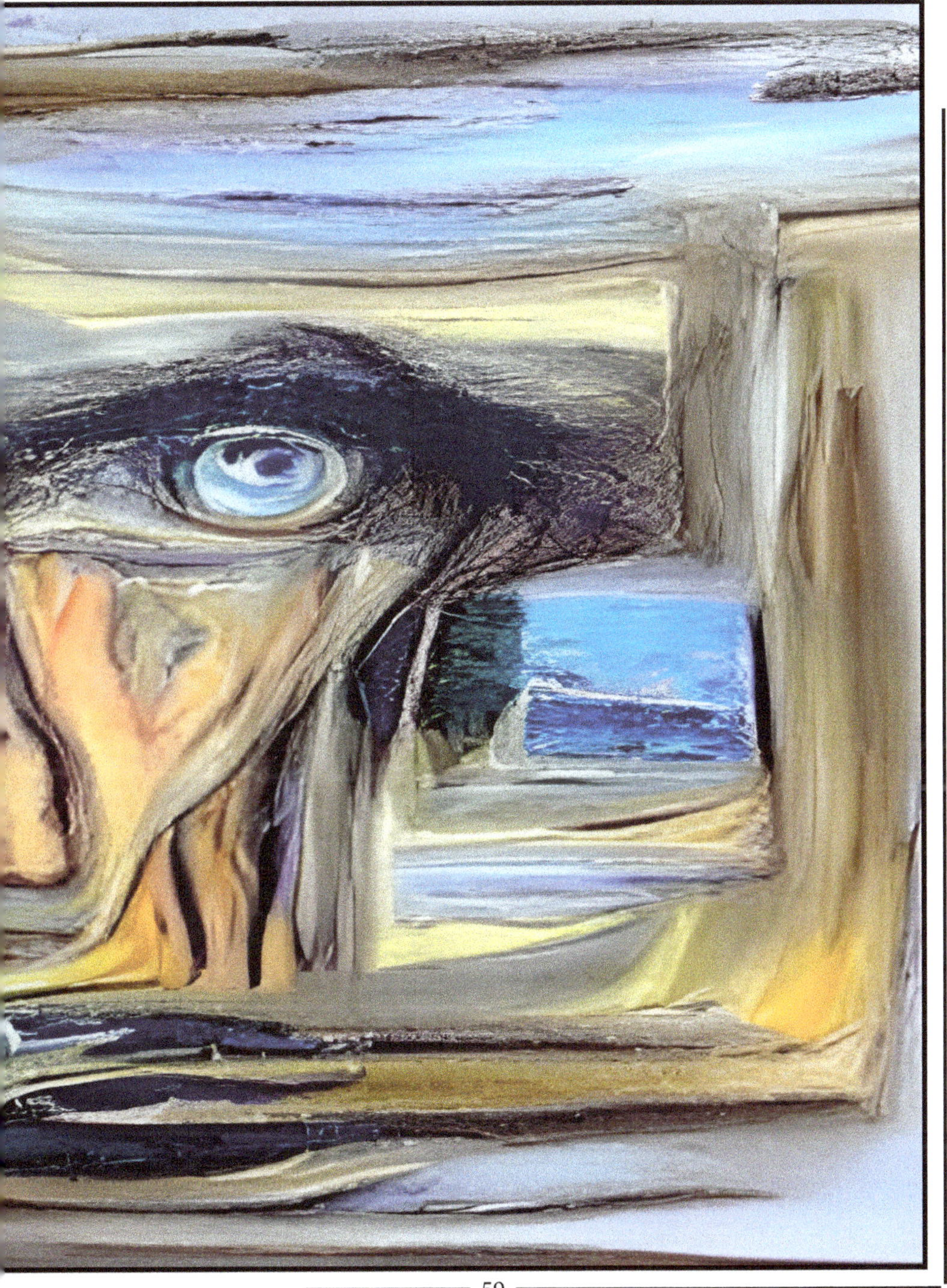

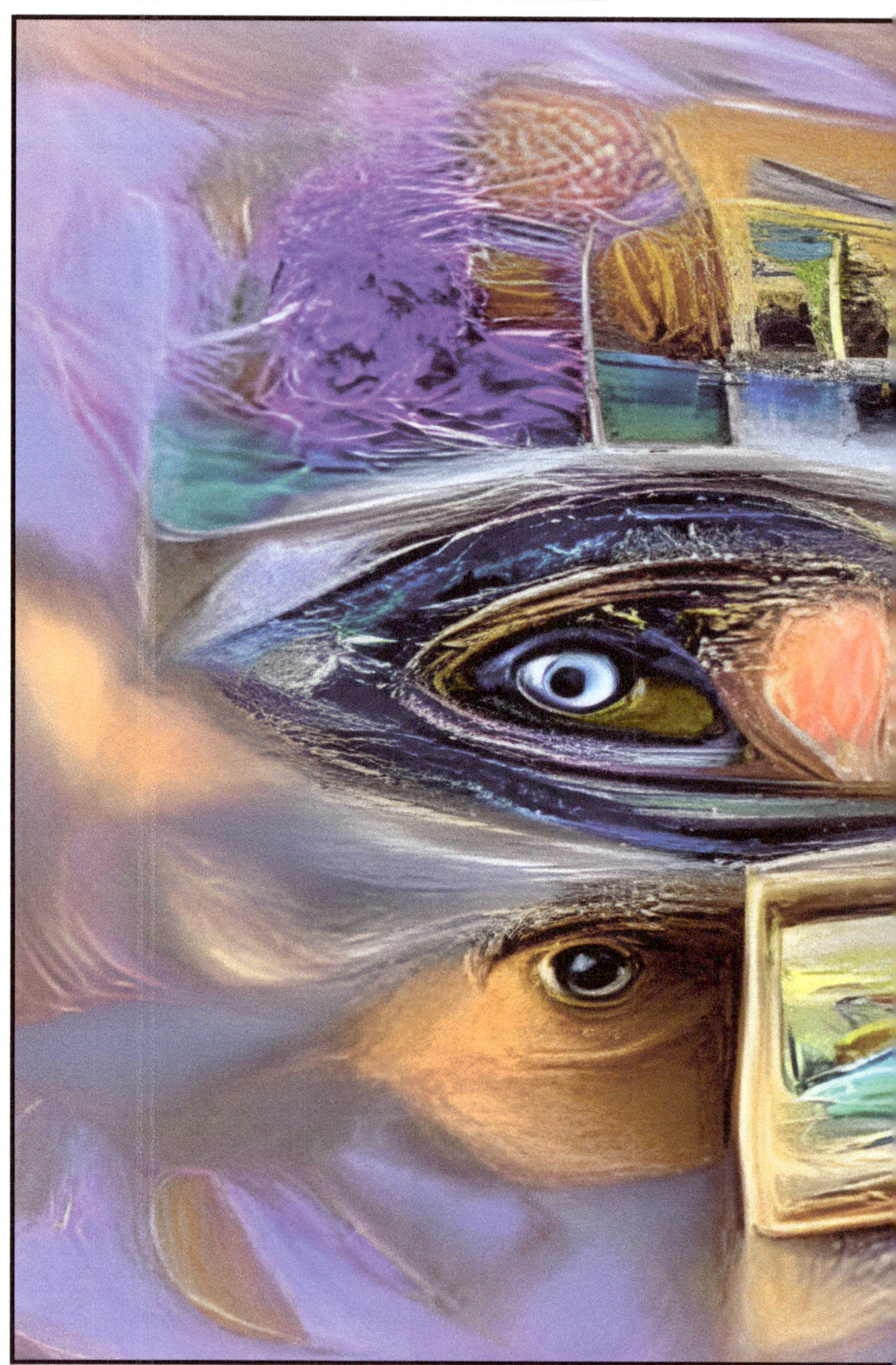

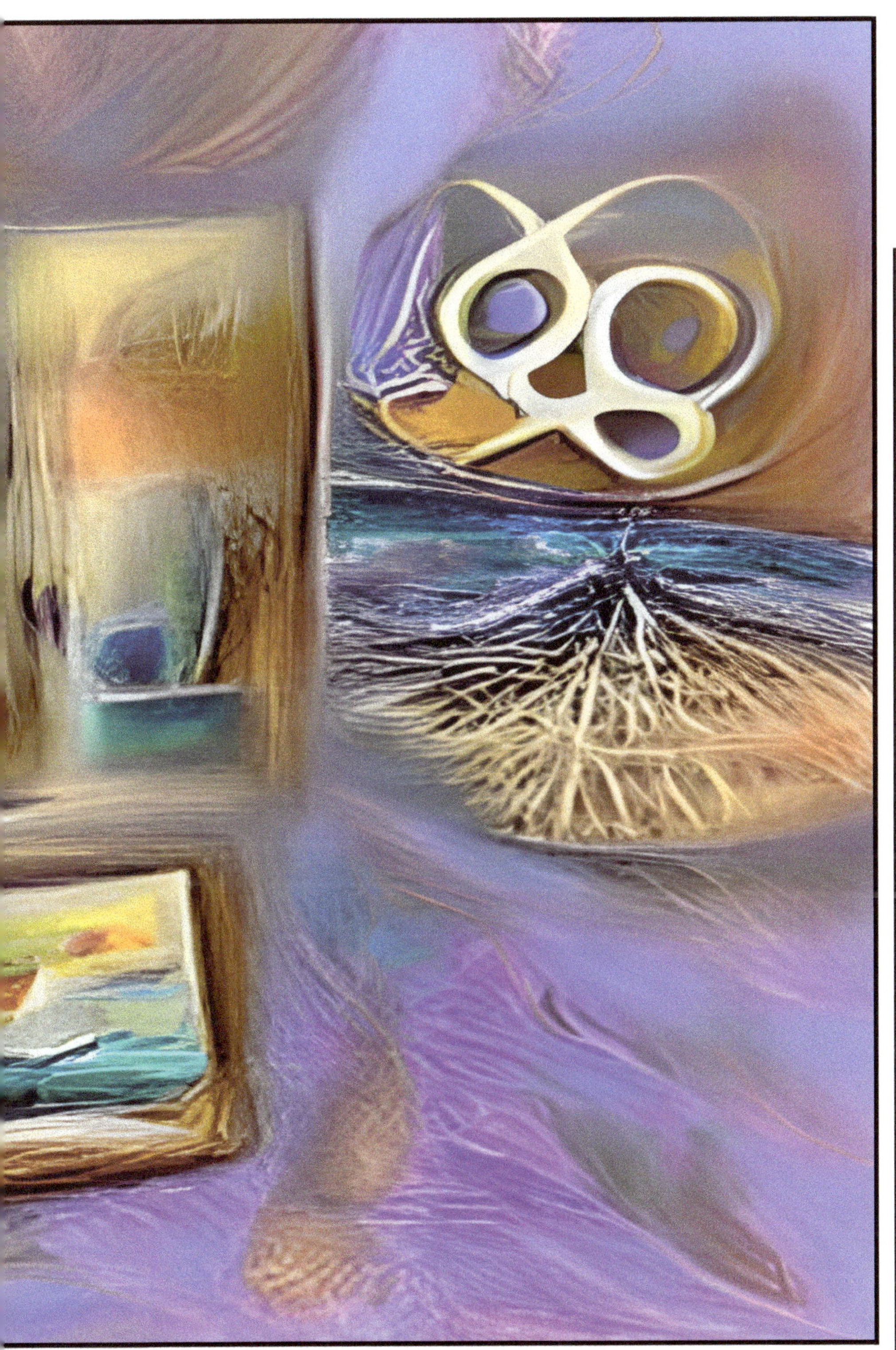

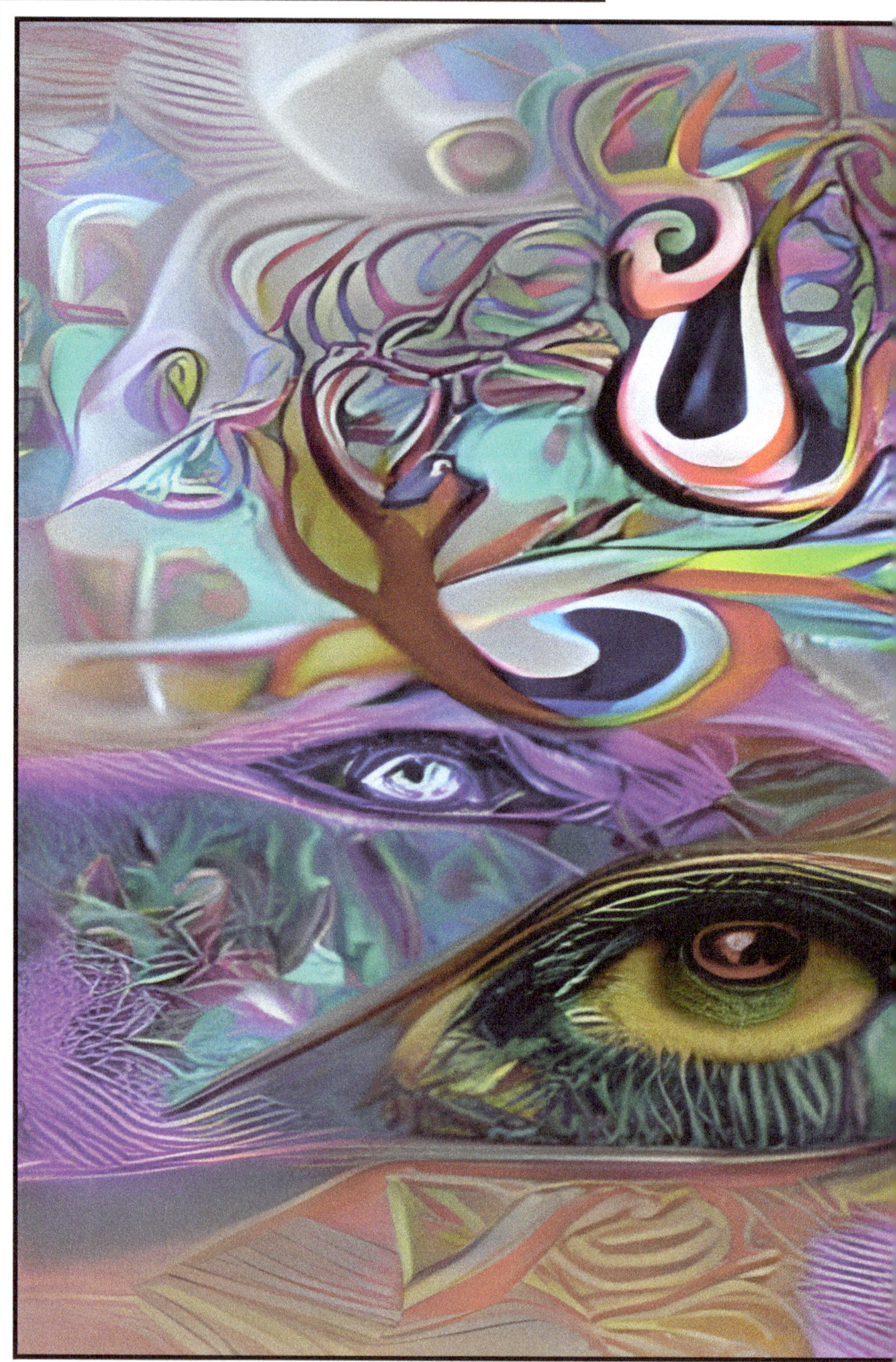

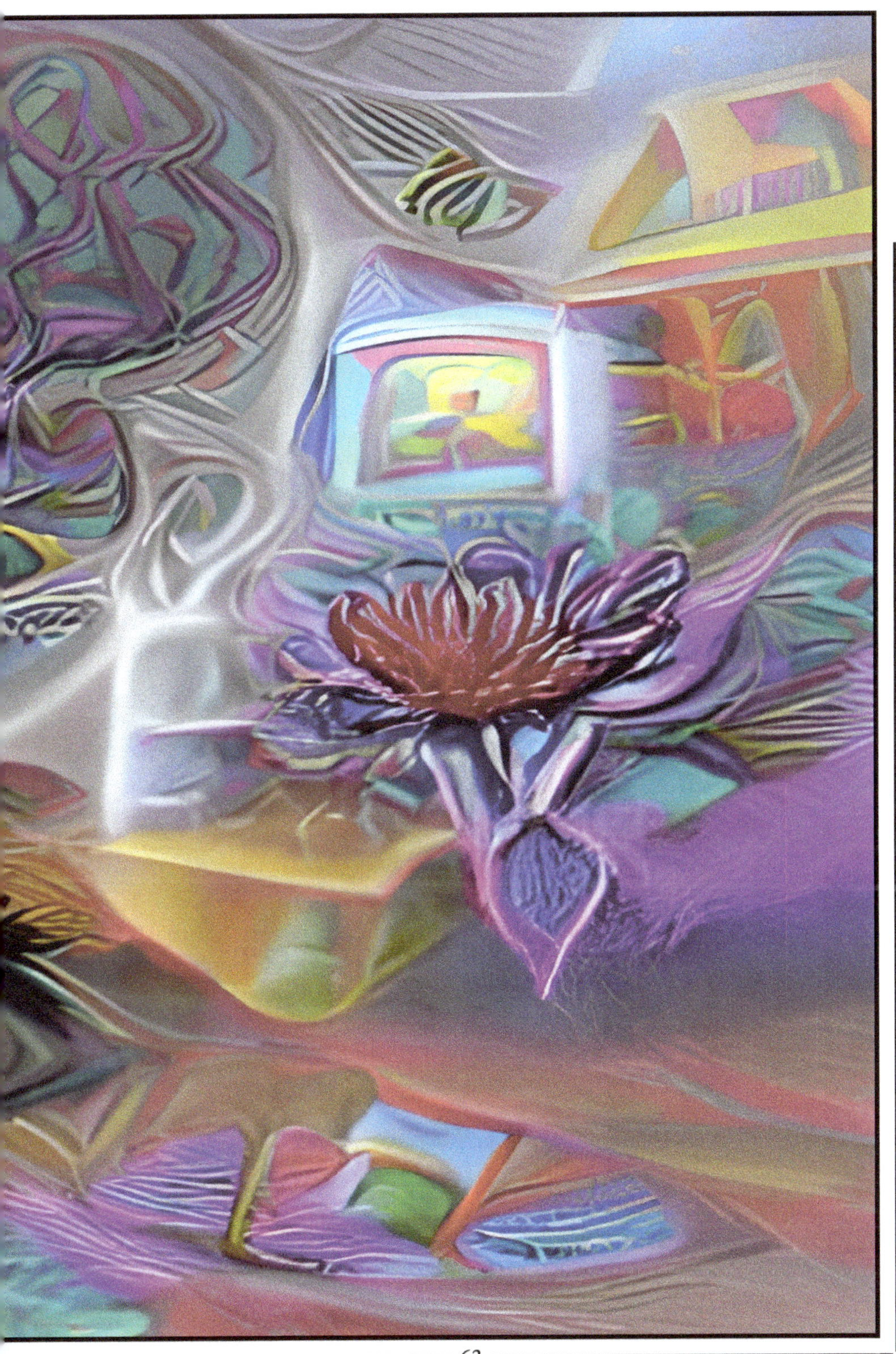

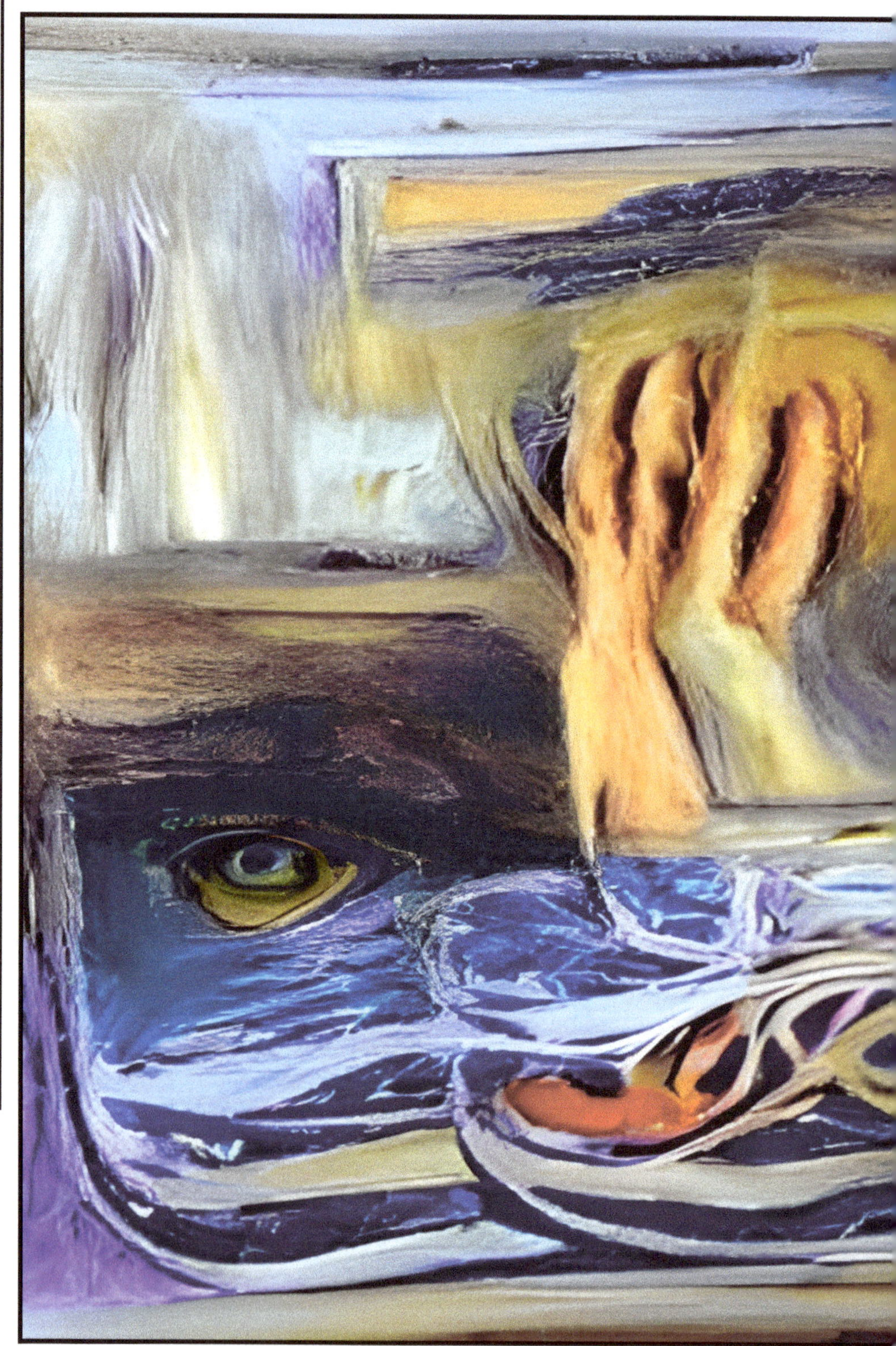

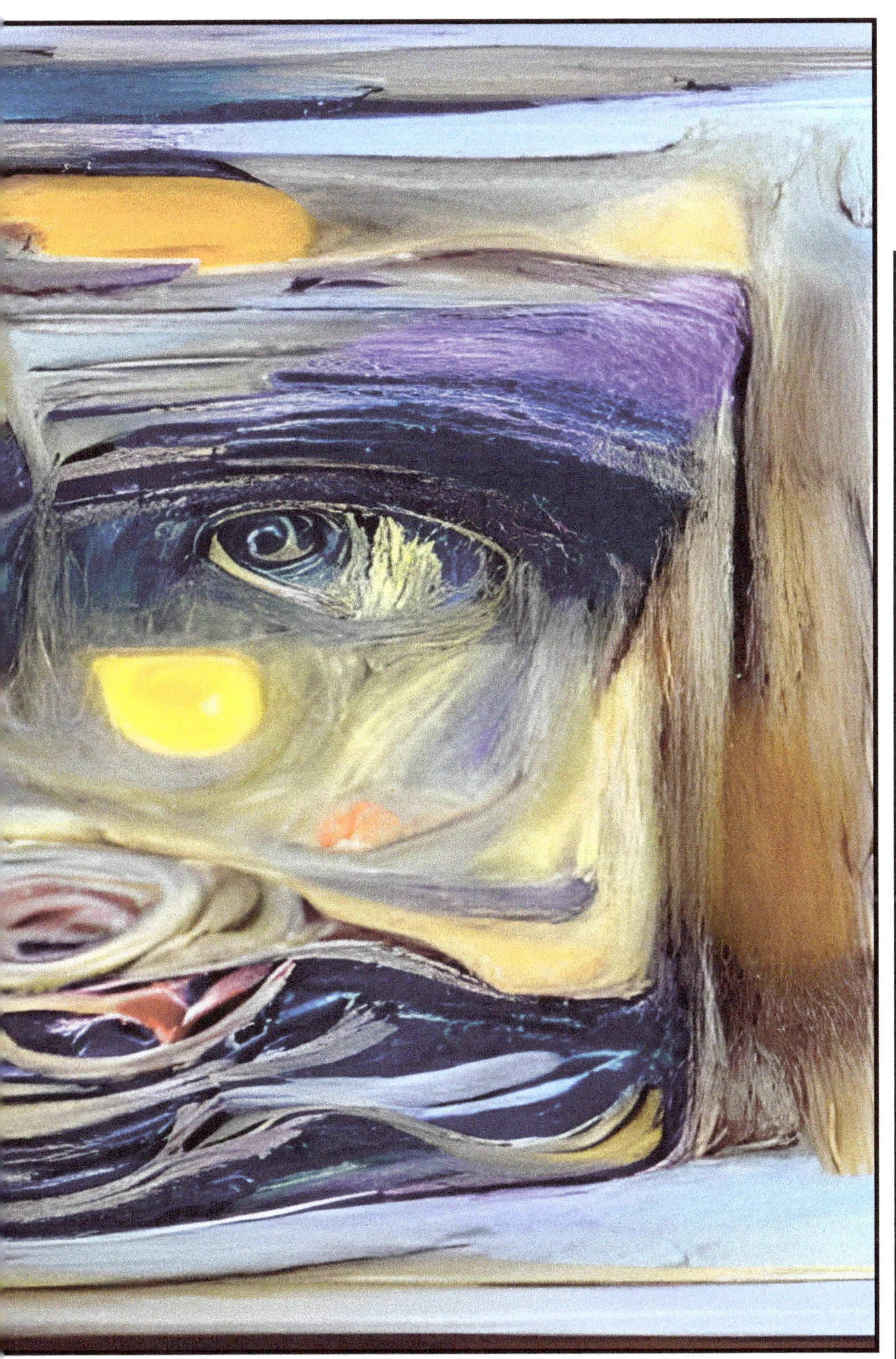

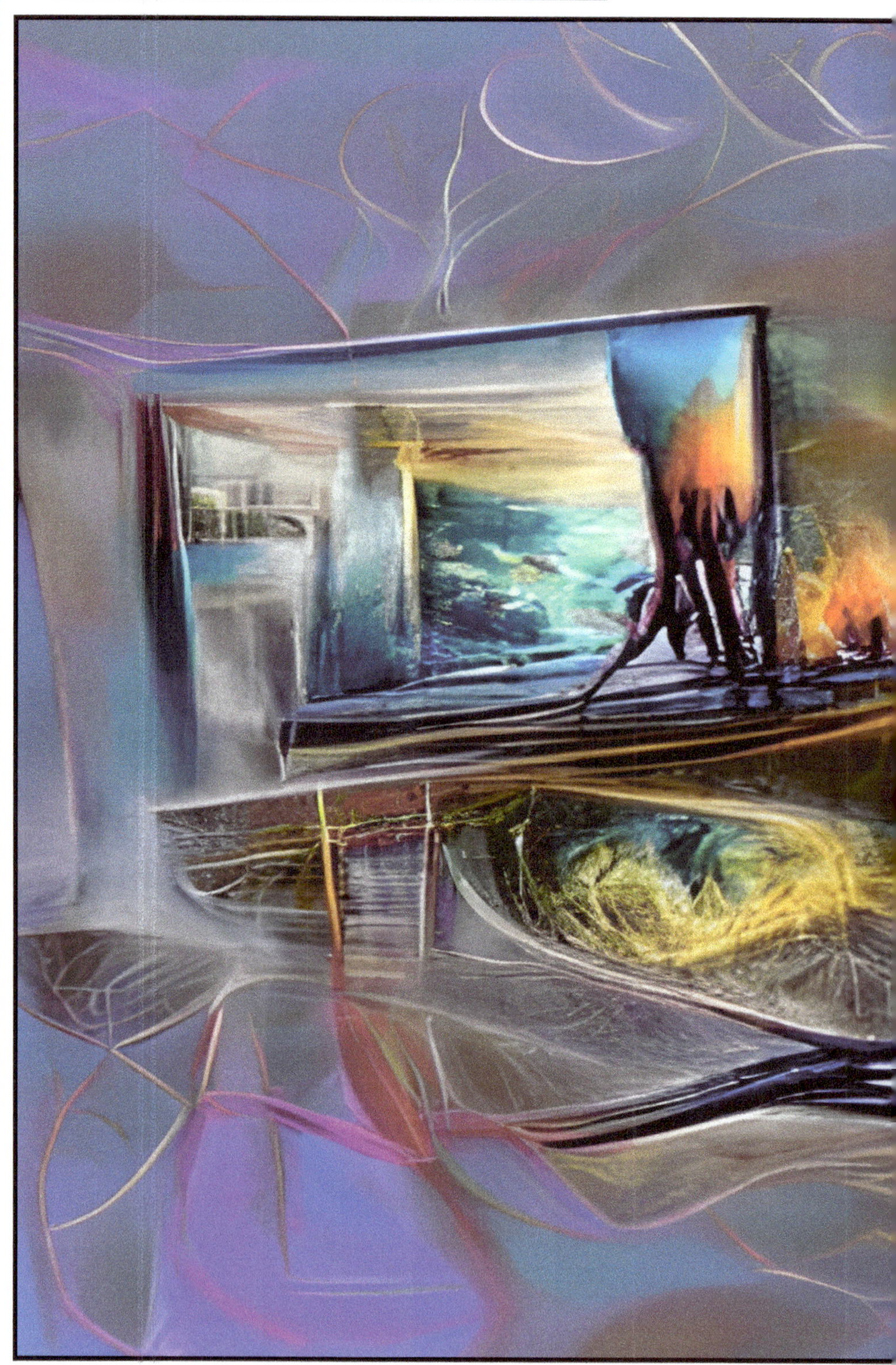

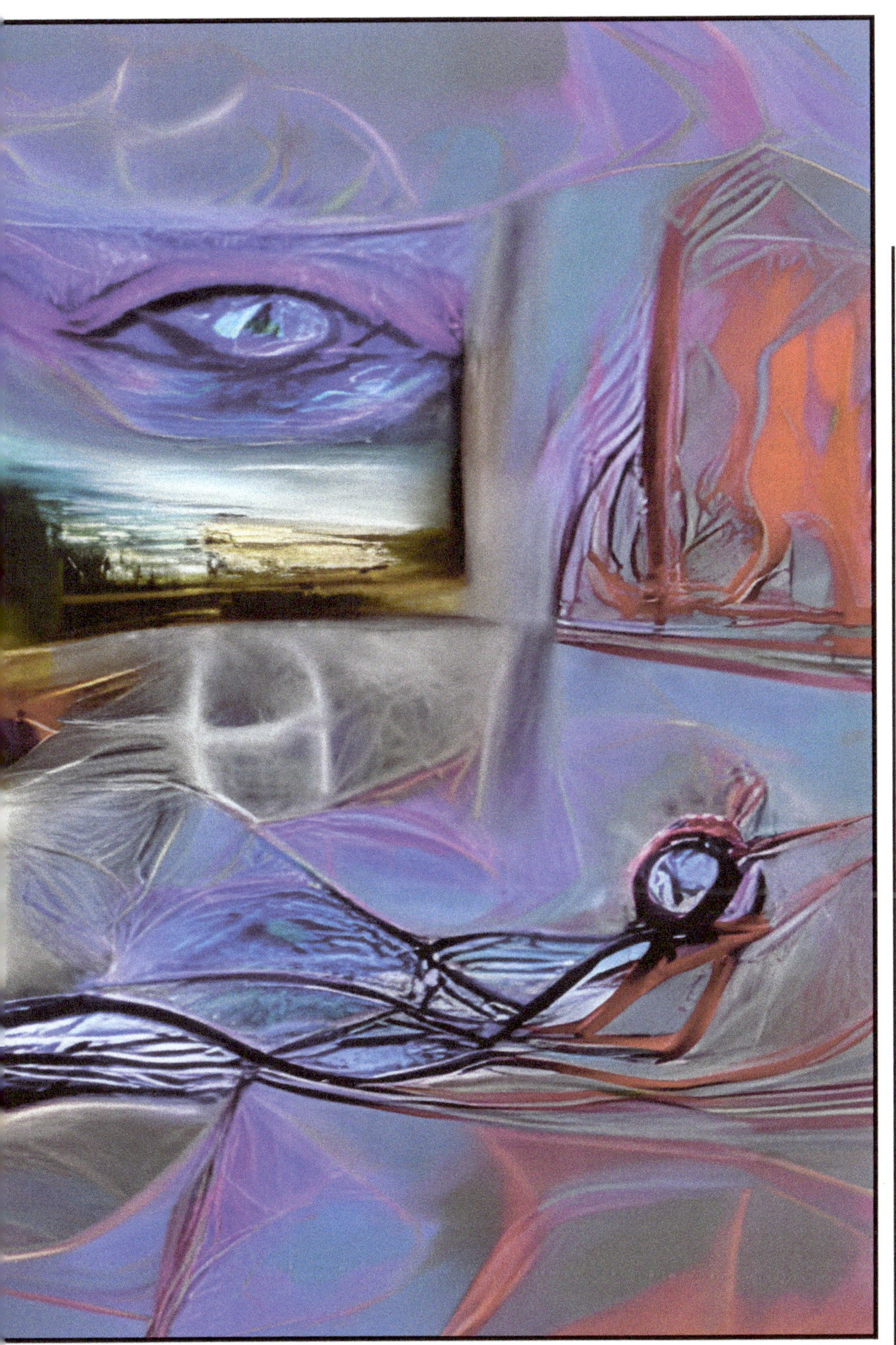

Freedom Sounds

Alexandra Cox

I came home during hunting season,
7am punched by a brief string of
gunshots, like footsteps,
bringing me to the blind,
rammed with stalks,
frayed gun shells, empties,
fox holes; running close,
dogs pacing over dormant lives
thrumming beneath men,
their sons behind them,
pulling decoys, leaning into the
Tidewater wind, dots of camo
against winter corn.

Geese, liberated from hunters,
fly over them, their shrieks,
almost gentle, shifting,
then gone, though a rumble
rolls over the creek, thunderous.

Dad said it was munitions:
covert, sublime sounds
traveling over water, air
cooling the explosions
over the Chesapeake,
from Aberdeen.

The military tell us they are
'sounds of freedom,' proving the
ground, while the stands
roll up along the avenues,
inauguration coming,
Kabul still beckoning
toward Washington,
'A small town seethes
after learning one of its own
says he joined Capitol's mob,'
from Aberdeen, a hunter's son.

Red dress.

Emily Rosier

He knocked at 3 a.m with no promises, we had a drink,
he took my dress, the wall he pinned me up against was cloud,
I disappeared and left my body, to a sandy beach, a warm bed, toast and honey,
my mum's home made bread,
the smell of rain around my apartment, 23 floors up,
when the air turned white,
and when it passed I burnt that dress,
and I pretended.
I can't pretend now, so I wear that dress, everyday, although it's ashes.

Dear God, the Boy Isn't Alright

Asya Wilson

Sip. Gulp. And Mother's gone to bed after completing her nightly routine: drinking a generous glass of wine and taking two sleeping pills while you are in the shower. Your son has also gone to bed.

It's around this time that you get on your knees, place your elbows on the edge of the mattress, press your palms together, lower your head. An odd sight, yes: a large lump of a man slumped over, bare besides a pair of boxers, mumbling alone in a dark room.

"The boy isn't alright," you whisper. Do you whisper because you are worried you will wake Mother or because you are ashamed of what you are confessing before God, or is it something else?

"I've tried and I've tried," you say. "How do I steer him on the right path?" Your palms are now raised, facing upward, steadily shaking in rhythm to a worship song only you hear.

A moment of silence comes next. Were you intently listening to an answer from God, or were you waiting for an answer that never came, or were you simply thinking of how to continue, or did a sudden stomach pain perhaps make you stop and breathe in and out for a moment until a passing of gas relieved the pressure, or was it something else? Eventually, you continue.

"I didn't raise him this way, Lord. It's got to be his mother, or the school, or his friends, or the things they show on television; it's got to be something," you say, shaking your head. You continue this way for a while, until you to go to bed.

"Amen."

You pray like this every night for your boy, sometimes more. He hasn't been alright for a long time. You perhaps first noticed when the boy's first grade pictures came in. He was wearing a purple pony print t-shirt that was meant for girls. Later you found out Mother had started letting him pick out his own clothes while shopping. You put a stop to that right away.

"You know damn well he shouldn't be wearing nothing like that," you told Mother. "He's a boy, dress him like one."

She listened, of course, only buying the blues and the greens and the browns, the football print tees and the athletic shorts and everything else that the boy models on the store posters would wear.

Or perhaps it wasn't his first grade pictures that made you really concerned but rather the time you caught him with his nails painted with nail polish he had traded his afternoon snack for with a desk mate at school. Or maybe it was his indifference toward sports, his lack of athletic drive that you and your father and your grandfather all had. Or was it that you noticed his friends have often tended to be girls or girly boys? Or did you rather see it over time in the little things: in the certain way he sits, the manner he walks about, the way he looks at certain things compared to other things, in all the ways he isn't like you?

No matter, you've since made helping your son overcome his problem the most important thing in your life. In the process you've come to feel you are something of a doctor, or a teacher, or at the least a savior of sorts, not in a prideful or proud way, but with a sense of duty and responsibility. Not God himself, but nonetheless something along the lines of God? You've therefore taken it upon yourself to speak his wisdom and act on his behalf when speaking isn't enough.

Go get the belt.

It's true that you've tried many things to help your son. For several years now you've sent him to summer camps for boys. *To toughen him up. To help him find his true self.* When he's not away, you try to spend quality time with him whenever you can: taking him to your office to see you work, watching Thursday night football together, playing catch outside or going fishing, praying to God hand in hand during Sunday's morning service.

Always, you think he is getting a little better. Always, until he doesn't seem to be anymore.

Go get the belt.

More than anything you are concerned for your boy and what will become of his future.

Your heart aches. It's why you pray. Why you do what you do. For him, for the family. You think you'll just have to work harder.

God, I will not falter. I will persevere.

And despite everything, you are grateful for your son. You feel some higher power has added these challenges to your life only so that you can overcome them. As a boy, your father always told you, what makes a real man is not the challenges he has avoided, but the challenges he has overcome and survived. You know your son is not at fault but rather you, for having not saved him yet.

Father, forgive me for allowing my son to become this way. Thank you for your patience. Thank you for your wisdom.

You pray to God and thank him, thank him for the opportunity to right the wrongs of others. Thank him for the opportunity to save your own flesh and blood, your precious son from sin. You never doubt that you are blessed.

God is good. Yes, all the time. Thank you, God.

Still, it hasn't been easy on you, trying to get your son on the right path. But you don't give up because you know it is all in *his* plan. You know what you must do as his father. You must teach him right from wrong. Cure his any and every disease. Save him. Teacher. Doctor. Savior. God?

You made a promise to him after all, when he was just a baby. The time you first held the tiny new life in your hands and said, "You don't know me yet, but I am your dad, and I will take care of you, always."

Daddy is here. Shh. Shh. Don't cry, I'm here. Always.

So once again, when night comes after another tiresome and difficult day, despite every bone in your body telling you to go to bed—*rest, sleep, forget about your troubles, you've done all that you could do*—you bend down on your knees, elbows on the bed, hands joined, head down, and you start: "Dear God."

Dolphin Dies—Owner Turns to Alcohol

Dustin Hyman

Reagan Thorndike, 49 years old, was found dead in his home last Thursday, floating in two feet of putrid sake (rice alcohol). His pet dolphin was also discovered, half decomposed, inside the home. Authorities knew to search the house when neighbors called about the stench. Lulu Simms lived across the street from Mr. Thorndike for 12 years—she described the smell as "overtly sexual and fishy." Mr. Thorndike's Facebook profile boasts a degree in "Marine Biology" from "Idaho Marine Institute," but this staff writer was unable to find any indication of said school.

Local zoologist Sharen Seth identified the marine mammal as a Tursiops, more commonly known as Bottlenose Dolphin. Mr. Thorndike's various social media profiles chronicle his history with the animal, going back seven years, when the pet was acquired illegally in Tijuana, Mexico. An Instagram post from June of 2016 provides the first mention of the dolphin's name: "Slick Rick."

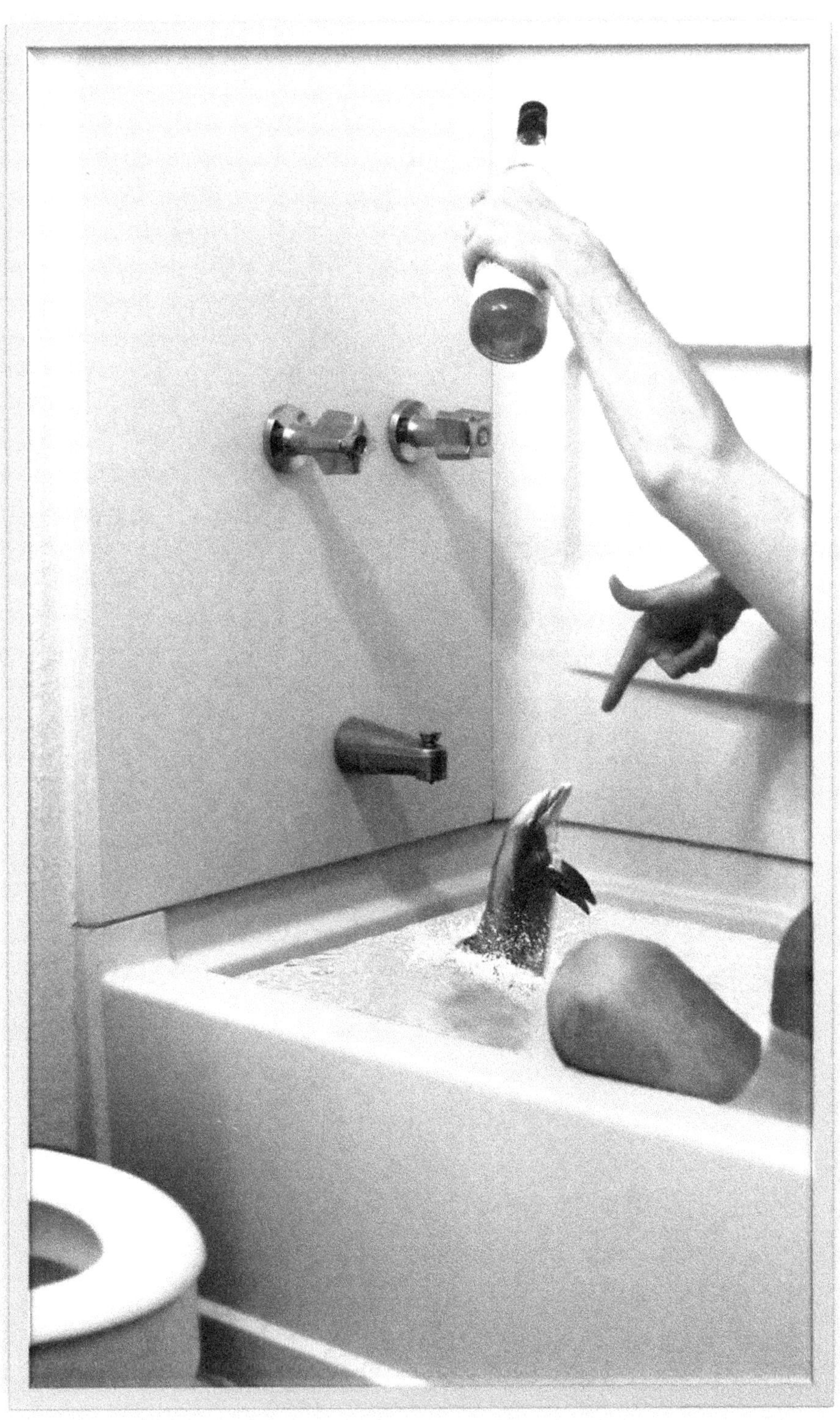

A 2017 Reddit.com thread under the heading "Keepin Dolphin Alive in Captivity" confirms that Mr. Thorndike (referring to himself as "Big-Rick" in this chatroom) was searching the internet for information regarding saltwater aquariums: "Anybody know how much salt to dilute into fresh water to make a livable dolphin habitat?"

What follows is a torrent of jokes. But one internet blogger (@Doodle_Poodle) did offer a formula: "nine-to-one." Whether Mr. Thorndike used this crude equation to model a home for Slick-Rick is still a matter of speculation.

According to the expertise of Ms. Seth, who was hired by the Atascadero police department to conduct an autopsy, "the poor animal could have died from numerous things." However, it is her professional opinion that Slick-Rick likely succumbed to "malnutrition and mental abuse."

In July of 2021, Mr. Thorndike's social media posts took a turn for the worse. He described his home as "a flooded hell" (Facebook). Neighbors noticed changes in behavior. "Every night they'd go at each other for hours," said Kyle Garner, a longtime resident of the neighborhood. Garner went on to say, "Sometimes I didn't know who was yelling and who was crying. They seemed to mirror one another."

Doris Deckles, an ex-girlfriend of Mr. Thorndike, described the dolphin as "jaded" and resentful of "deplorable living conditions." When asked why her ex-boyfriend purchased a dolphin in the first place: "It's because he saw a documentary on YouTube where a lady gave a pet dolphin hand-jobs." The video referenced, *Stroking My Dolphin*, is a biography of Margaret Howe Lovatt, a NASA-Funded researcher who serially relieved her friend Peter (also a bottlenose dolphin) during the 1960s.

According to Deckles, the documentary film ended their relationship because Mr. Thorndike became "fixated with the sex organs of marine mammals." Deckles concluded the interview by saying, "The sick [expletive] would have preferred a walrus. But they don't sell [expletive] walruses in Tijuana!"

Gump Seafood confirmed making deliveries to the residence during a four-year period, from 2018 to 2021. According to their records, Slick-Rick required approximately 90 pounds of frozen mackerel every two weeks. Whether Mr. Thorndike was supplementing the diet with other foods is unclear, but containers of "Complete Fish" vitamins were found inside the residence.

Regardless of the cause, when Slick-Rick died, Mr. Thorndike went off the deep-end. A toxicology report noted that Mr. Thorndike was "literally drowning in alcohol." The nine-page report goes on to reveal that Mr. Thorndike's Blood Alcohol Content (BAC) was around 3.3 at the time of his death. California motorists can expect to be jailed for Driving Under the Influence (DUI) when their breath reveals a BAC of .09 or higher.

During a recent phone interview, detective Donny Lebowski explained how Mr. Thorndike was able to transform his two-bedroom home into a saltwater aquarium, and following the death of Slick Rick, an alcohol fermentation chamber: "It really boiled down to Flex-Seal, Duct-Tape, and mental illness." Officer Lebowski described how the made for TV product, "Flex-Seal," was used to prevent seepage and leakage, "from floor to window-sills," providing the porpoise with approximately 2.7 feet of habitat (water). "When the dolphin expired," Officer Lebowski notes in his report, "Thorndike went from pet owner to Sake maker."

Sierra Nevada Brew-Master John Beck Johnson offered his take on the situation via email: "Although I've never brewed Sake, I know how it's done. I've been making booze for 34 years. Knowing that this man was found belly up in a brew of 19% alcohol, and knowing that his home held nearly 36,000 gallons of filthy booze, this crazy asshole would have needed approximately 2,200 pounds of rice...I won't bore you with the math."

Mr. Thorndike's neighbor, Ms. Deckles, recalls two palettes of rice arriving from Amazon following the death of Slick Rick: "I thought he was gonna donate it. But he walked around the house and poured rice into each window. He was wearing a turquoise bathrobe." Brew-Master Johnson estimated that it would have taken two weeks for the Dolphin habitat to become alcoholic, and when it did, Thorndike's behavior shifted from eccentric to psychotic.

Ms. Deckles reports seeing Uber-Eats vehicles deliver Burger King and Taco Bell to his home. According to her, "Thorndike would open his bedroom window and make the

transactions. He never had a shirt on." She went on to mention that, "Thorndike would lean his ass out of the bathroom window and shit twice a day. He was a fascinating individual. The only thing regular about Thorndike were the poops."

Authorities found the decomposing body of Slick Rick floating inside a closet. Ms. Seth (aforementioned Marine Biologist) noted that the animal was extremely small for its age, "likely due to confinement."

A private funeral for Mr. Thorndike will be held at the Chappell of the Roses this Sunday. His final Tweet: "News will shout: *Man Killed Dolphin!* I bought Rick a blowfish just to get him high. He loved it. What's the nicest thing y'all have done for a Dolphin? My best friend died. At least I tried."

The Mockery of Light

Image by Megan Stephenson

Poetry by Devon Balwit

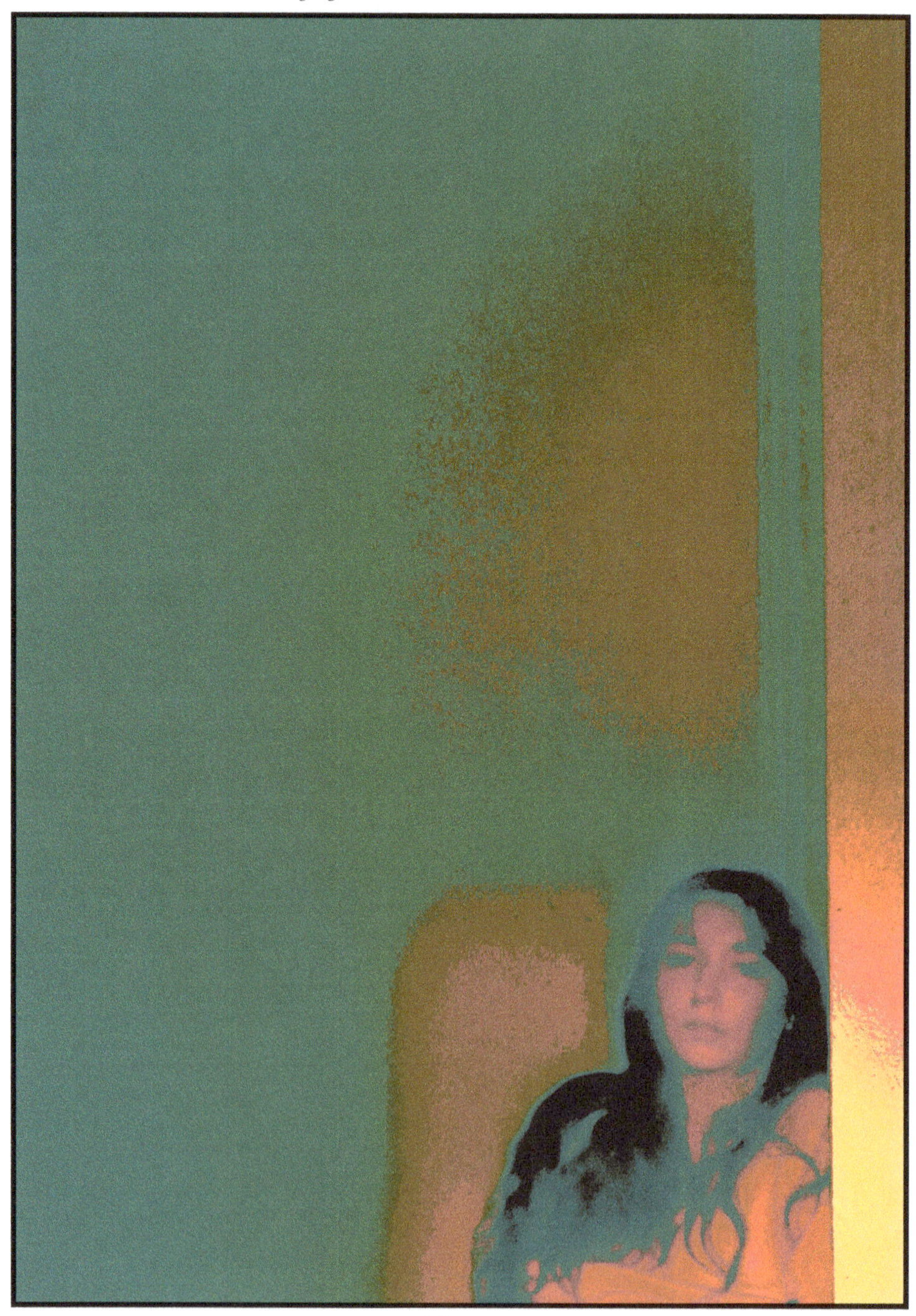

Blinking doesn't help. You, who thought
yourself so obviously [t]here, are nothing
more than afterimage, your youth-
ful beauty the good bones beneath the rot-
ten exterior. When your mother used to swear
she felt your age, you snorted. Now, you try
to follow your grown children out the door.
Gently, they lead you back, uninvited
to whatever after-party beckons.
There in the confines of your longing,
you dream a tap against the glass.
All that's left is to knuckle your eyes
and feed upon the mockery of light.

In Order Of Appearance:

Margie B. Klein has worked in southern Nevada for 30 years, and has been writing about travel and nature for just as long. Her certifications include Professional Tourist Guide, Interpretive Guide, and Environmental Educator. She is a fellow with the International League of Conservation Writers, and has won an award in writing from The Wildlife Society.

Adrienne is the New York Times Bestselling author of Pride Over Pity. She holds a BA in Journalism from Hofstra University. Her other creative endeavors include music and writing, with a particular passion for traveling the world to see her favorite bands.
@adriennewenner

Emily Griffin is a poet, librarian, and food enthusiast from Brooklyn, New York. Her poetry borrows from both the confessional and surrealist poetry traditions. Her work has appeared in Allegory Ridge's anthology, *Aurora *and is forthcoming in *Abandoned Mine*.

Josh Feit's poetry has been published in Spillway, Vallum, the Halcyone Literary Review, and Change Seven among other journals. He was a finalist for the 2021 Wolfson Chapbook Poetry Prize and the 2019 Lily Poetry Prize. He was shortlisted for the 2020 Vallum Award for Poetry and won Honorable Mention. His first chapbook, "The Night of Electric Bikes," is forthcoming from Finishing Line Press. He is the speechwriter for Seattle's regional transit agency.

Anna Hillary is an educator, writer, and editor. She loves plants and animals, humid summers and snowy winters, and calls both Buenos Aires, Argentina and La Crosse, Wisconsin home. Anna is based between the two cities, where she is currently writing her doctoral dissertation on high school student activism. Her instagram is @annazyxo

Artist Justin Snyder presents a fascinating and unique approach to the California beaches. Through his camera lenses, he is capturing the surfers - people who are challenging themselves to catch the wave, tame it, and finally ride it. Sandy beaches in Justin's works play an interesting role; it becomes a surface, which sometimes is being filled with the resting surfers; it becomes the beach bar location or just a symbol, marking the landscape line. The photographer is putting all his attention into the waves, the bodies of the surfers and that hardly describable feeling, which is being felt when a man approaches the strength of nature. As the artist states, he is considering his works as a "little old school with a touch of abstract style."
He doesn't move his camera away from the oil rigs, which also symbolizes human-built monstrosity; Justin captures them in complete stillness, while being surrounded by always dynamic ocean. All his surfing series is a love story to the ocean and to people who tame the waves.
Instagram: @justinsnyderphoto

Nancy Klepsch has been published in many online and print publications, and has exhibited or curated public poetry installations throughout the Capital Region of Upstate NY; some of these installations received grant awards from Breathing Lights, the New York State Council on the Arts via its community-based arts grants program, the City of Troy, NY and the Albany International Airport. god must be a boogie man is her first published book of poems.

Walter Weinschenk is an attorney, writer and musician. Until a few years ago, he wrote short stories exclusively but now divides his time equally between poetry and prose. Walter's writing has appeared in a number of literary publications including the Carolina Quarterly, Lunch Ticket (Amuse-Bouche), Cathexis Northwest Press, Beyond Words, The Gateway Review, The Raw Art Review and others. His work is due to appear in forthcoming issues of the Iris Literary Journal, The Banyan Review, Lighthouse Weekly, Sheepshead Review and Sand Hills Literary Magazine. Walter lives in a suburb just outside Washington, D. C.

Margo Griffin is a Boston, MA area urban public school educator and has worked in the field of education for almost thirty years. She is a divorced mother of two daughters and to the love of her life and best rescue dog ever, Harley.

My name is Catherine Lieser and I am a Berlin based photographer. My focus is on the values of self-empathy and self-determination. I work independently and on my own initiative as well as on behalf of companies and organizations. My comissioned work is used for press and marketing matters. I show my work in solo and group exhibitions and they are published in international photography magazines. Art prints of selected pieces are available to buy at UPHK.

GJ Gillespie is a collage artist living on Whidbey island north of Seattle. Winner of 17 awards, his art has appeared in 52 regional shows. The artists he admire tap unconscious feelings of longing for existential meaning that emerge from cultural icons. In his view abstraction should be more than pleasing design. Instead, art should evoke connotations that permit the viewer to experience a sense of wonder, awe and new perspectives of being.
A favorite quote: The world is but a canvas to our imagination. -- Henry David Thoreau.

Greg Sendi is a Chicago writer and former fiction editor at Chicago Review. His career has included broadcast and trade journalism as well as poetry and fiction. In the past year, his work has appeared or been accepted for publication in a number of literary magazines and online outlets, including Apricity, Beyond Words, The Briar Cliff Review, Burningword, Clarion, CONSEQUENCE, Great Lakes Review, The Masters Review, Plume, Pulp Literature, San Antonio Review, and upstreet.

Biff Rushton is a writer, singer/songwriter, traveler, music/word addict, father/husband, and a sixth generation East Texan. He dropped out of college to play music, but ended up having enough daughters to complete a WNBA lineup and working in the TX oilfield. As a poet he is self taught, but what he lacks in accredited hours, he makes up for with a vivid passion and a deep respect for the craft. His debut poetry collection will be released in late 2021 by Edyn Books, a small, newly formed press in Austin.
His IG is solbluesol

Zephyr Z is a computer programmer from Kearns, Utah who uses code to generate modern art. He is a self-taught artist using a Generative Adversarial Network (GAN) in his creative art process.
As an independent fun-loving soul, he is a Computer Scientist who loves to create new generative art algorithms, combining them with live performance. In this way, his emotions and feelings become a part of the experience.
He is also exploring his interests in creating modern computer-based art. He gets most of his innovative and creative inspirations from Programming.
Since artificial intelligence is already used to generate faces, music, and even poetry. He wanted to discover if it could be used to create art that looks like a human painted it.
The end results are an ever-evolving process of creation and destruction. Each workpiece is unique, with its own story and personality. In this way, he's able to create stunning and unique patterns.

Alexandra Cox is a sociologist working between the US and the UK.

For as long as she can remember, Emily has kept sketchpads and notebooks, filled with the pages of her life, in words and images.
She loves finding one of her past books and flipping through it.
There is both surprise and familiarity in what she finds inside.
The poems, and the pictures, transport her right back to where she was and how she felt, the day she wrote or sketched them.
They are evocative, in so many ways.
They remind her of moments of her life, sometimes joyful, sometimes painful, and occasionally they surprise her by recalling the depth of feeling she experienced, and the strange recognition of herself, as she was then, changed over the years, but the same in many ways.
She will always write, and draw and paint.It is her way of expressing deep joy, terrible sadness, or just the strange and wonderful and agonising and beautiful aspects of being alive.
It has always been a very private part of her life, until now.
She has not felt brave enough to expose herself, the most secret, real ways she sees the world, and feels about life, or about herself.

However, she has long hoped to create a book which, like one of her sketchpads, is an intriguing
and exciting, thought provoking, visual and verbal feast , which, perhaps would be as interesting to
others, as looking through her sketchpads and the wealth of thoughts and feelings they provoke is, to
her.
She hopes it might inspire emotion, stir the senses, perhaps prompt recognition of certain feelings
or experiences.she hopes it moves people, and makes them thoughtful.
So, here they are....some of her poems, in this case...private for so many years...her heart and soul on
paper.
She hopes they make people feel.

Asya writes from Washington State. Her writing has been published in Inkwell Journal, The Noncon-
formist Magazine, and elsewhere.

Megan Stephenson is a working artist located in Boston MA. She specializes in mixed media art,
inclusive of painting, photography, and the mixing of both. She focuses on her sense of identity and
the struggle to perform to societal standards, and cope with the strains of life as a disabled, queer
and female identifying person. The photos she has submitted here, are demonstrative of her fluidity
in self expression, and how her self expression is a constant flowing self realization, abstracted by
the ideas and labels we put on eachother. If you wish to view more of her work you may follow her on
instagram @art_by_megans.

Devon Balwit walks in all weather. Her most recent collections are Rubbing Shoulders with the
Greats [Seven Kitchens Press 2020] and Dog-Walking in the Shadow of Pyongyang [Nixes Mate
Books, 2021]. https://pelapdx.wixsite.com/devonbalwitpoet

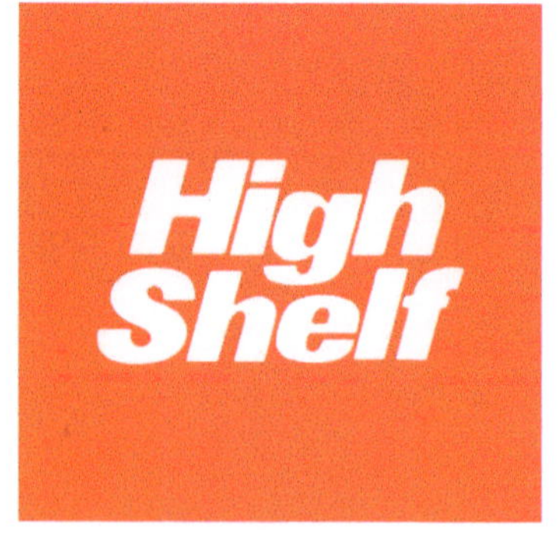

Highshelfpress.com